You're Just a Keystroke Away From Your Most Successful Sales and Marketing Program Ever

If you want to drive profitable business plans— if you want to determine the actual cost of Sales and Marketing and the projected revenue before you spend any money—then you want *The Buck Starts Here* software program for Windows.®

The *Buck Starts Here* software allows you to create, implement and manage a Sales and Marketing business plan that is focused on driving toward your revenue and profit targets. *The Buck Starts Here* software helps you:

- Determine the actual cost of Sales and Marketing and compare it to the revenue expected prior to spending any money on Sales and Marketing

- Determine how much revenue you need to drive and how many customers must buy (by product type) in order for you to be successful

- Profile your ideal prospect and analyze your customer's Buying Cycle

- Determine your own Sales Cycle (what you will say, do and measure) to get that customer to buy

- Map out all of the key players in the customer's Buying Cycle

The *Buck Starts Here* software program requires a Windows-compatible spreadsheet program and either Microsoft Word or WordPerfect word processing software. The cost is only $19.95.

For More Information or to Order, call 1-888-420-3232

PINN·FLEX

Pinnaflex Educational Resources, Inc.
Cincinnati, Ohio
www.pinnaflex.com
e-mail: jsitlington@fuse.net

ABOUT PINNAFLEX

Pinnaflex Educational Resources, Inc., produces high-quality, timely, and exceptional-value products and online courseware for improving corporate, individual, and executive learning and development. Our products are prepared by leading content providers in business, academe, government, and the nonprofit sector. Pinnaflex integrates new technologies and proven content to achieve highly interactive anytime, anywhere learning. Whether content is delivered in hard type on the page or through a computer monitor, Pinnaflex has devoted its resources to the ongoing perfection of on-demand learning.

AVAILABLE FROM PINNAFLEX

Practice-Driven Research in IT Management Series. The books in this series arise from the cutting-edge, practice-driven research conducted by leading scholars for the Advanced Practices Council (APC) of the Society for Information Management, International (SIM). These research projects focus on areas relevant to the successful management and use of information technology (IT) to achieve business objectives. They uncover best practices, innovations, and "next generation" thinking regarding critical topic areas in enterprisewide IT management.

Crossing Boundaries: *The Deployment of Global IT Solutions* (Collins/Kirsch). This book, based on extensive research, addresses the question of implementing and deploying global IT solutions to support worldwide business activities. It deals with these issues and more by analyzing the unique nature of global (versus domestic) IT solutions and identifying successful practices for deploying them.

Coping With Labor Scarcity in Information Technology: *Strategies and Practices for Effective Recruitment and Retention* (Agarwal/Ferratt). This book is about the effective management of the strategic HR/IT organizational resource. It asks and answers the question, "How can organizations more effectively find and keep productive IT professionals?" It is the culmination of over two years of primary field research conducted in several large and small corporations and illustrates what can be done to effectively address the IT labor shortage.

Repositioning the IT Organization to Enable Business Transformation (Brown/Sambamurthy). IT is proving to be a critical element of the value proposition of firms developing "sense and respond" capabilities, where competitive success is enabled by detecting fleeting windows of opportunity and quickly responding with winning products and services. This book explores the tactics and strategies that the CIOs of six firms used in repositioning their information services organization to support or shape the transformation of their business' strategies, capabilities, and competencies.

MANAGEMENT 2.0: *Managing in the 21st Century* (Duening). This book is predicated on the premise that the basic assumptions that had formed the foundation for the practice of management have been overturned. The idea that there is "one best way" to manage organizations has been replaced by contingency approaches. The idea that managers are responsible only for the "bottom line" has been replaced by a more expansive view that managers must be tactical as well as strategic.

The "age of technology" has introduced a "new economy," wherein organizations must face the reality that they are global entities, must embrace technology, and must exist within networks of strategic alliances, some long lasting, some short term. The book also deals extensively with successes and failures in E-Commerce and the ethical implications of the Internet, E-mail, and other tools of our age that impact managers.

To learn more about Pinnaflex's products and online capabilities, access our site at www.pinnaflex.com, *call us at 1-888-420-3232, or E-mail* jsitlington@fuse.net

THE BUCK STARTS HERE

Profit-Based Sales & Marketing Made Easy

MARY A. MOLLOY   MICHAEL K. MOLLOY

TRB Consulting Group, Inc.

(603) 236–4067
E-mail: trbinc@compuserve.com
www.pinnaflex.com/trb

PINN·FLEX

Pinnaflex Educational Resources, Inc.

Production Management: Kevin Cox, Custom Editorial Productions, Inc.
Production Coordination: JaNoel Lowe, Custom Editorial Productions, Inc.

This book was printed and bound by Malloy Lithographing, Inc., Ann Arbor, Michigan.

ISBN: 1-893673-04-9

TO OUR READERS:

Thank you for your interest in *The Buck Starts Here*. We wrote this book because clients repeatedly asked for books, job aids and training programs that focus on managing profit-driven sales and marketing strategies. This is exactly what our company, TRB Consulting Group, does. TRB provides training and consulting services in three critical areas of a company, namely:

- training Management teams to develop results-based, profit-driven sales and marketing strategies and programs
- teaching Sales organizations how to run their territories like a business— focusing on attaining business goals profitably while increasing customer satisfaction
- assisting companies in creating integrated customer-focused Sales and Marketing organizations—from product conception through customer satisfaction—that invest money instead of spending it

TRB offers a variety of innovative Sales, Marketing and Management training programs, including:

- *The Business of Marketing*
- *The Business of Selling Successfully—Run Your Territory Like a Business—for Both Your Direct Sales Force and Your Partners*
- *The Integrated Business of Sales and Marketing*
- *Creating Powerful and Persuasive Sales Messages*
- *Collecting Customer Data*
- *Managing Profit Driven Marketing and Sales Organizations*

As the principals of TRB, we have over 50 years of combined experience in Sales, Sales Management, Marketing Management, International Marketing and the training of Sales and Marketing Professionals. In the past three years, TRB Consulting Group has trained over 8,000 Sales, Marketing and Business professionals representing 50 countries, from very large corporations to very small companies.

One of our clients once said that "TRB is different from other consulting companies. TRB develops sales and marketing programs that fit our strategic objectives instead of trying to get us to change our strategies to fit their solutions." They were right. TRB is different and we are proud of it.

We would welcome your comments and questions about *The Buck Starts Here*. We hope you enjoy reading our book and using our software as much as we enjoyed writing them and teaching our methodology to others.

Mary and Mike Molloy
TRB Consulting Group, Inc.
P.O. Box 380
Waterville Valley, NH 03215
Phone: 603-236-4067
Fax: 603-236-4917
E-mail: trbinc@compuserv.com
Website: www.pinnaflex.com/trb

*This book is dedicated to
Jennifer, Christine, Jim and Michael.
You are wonderful kids and
we're lucky to have you.*

Acknowledgments

There are many people to whom we owe a big thank you.

Tanny Mann for being our first reviewer, encourager and book strategist. You were great. Thanks. Joan Jacobs for giving encouragement and feedback—not only on the book but on so many topics and areas of life. Ken Branco, Bob Wagner and Bob O'Rourke, for introducing us (directly or indirectly) to our publisher, Jim Sitlington. Jim Sitlington, for being a great publisher, adviser and a terrific person. Dave Todd for your marketing genius and Joe Ciccone for your support and love. Michael and Niki O'Rourke—how could we ever have done it all without your technical help? There's just no way. Bob Welch, Mary Welch and Rebecca Morris for providing true friendship, encouragement in times of strife and also for providing excellent feedback and business savvy. Michael O'Brien and Charlie King for their efforts in our Master Mind Title Creation Group. Tom Gross for being one of our biggest fans and confidants. Here's to "Legends" in the making. Thank you especially for our final title. Toni Lee Rudnicki, Karen Regan, Deb Svenson, Joanne Lutian, Bernie Mieth and Lee Rubenstein, who are also right up there in our mutual fan club. Thanks. John Gagliardo, Michael Gagliardo, Nancy and Joseph Gagliardo, Beatrice Napolitano, PJ and the Molloy family, Debbie Seter and Sydney Stevens for *always* being there for us. You guys are the best. What more can we say? Jack and Mary Gagliardo, not only for being great and loving parents, but for allowing the total disruption of your house for one week— where this book began. Microsoft Corp. for putting together such a great integrated office system—Microsoft Office. It is a pleasure to work with.

Contents

Introduction

We have had the opportunity to work with hundreds of Sales and Marketing organizations over the years. In fact we have trained well over 3,000 people representing 50 countries during the past three years. While our clientele includes many large corporations such as Microsoft, Motorola, and Digital Equipment Corporation, we have also worked with hundreds of small to medium-size companies. In our early careers, we were employees of companies in various Sales, Marketing and Management positions, so we have carried the briefcase, made our share of sales calls (including some we would like to forget) and developed, implemented and managed many sales and marketing programs.

More recently, we have been consulting with companies around the world, assisting them in developing common sense, easy-to-manage sales and marketing strategies. Regardless of company size, geography, market position or success, we have found that many companies fall into a consistent pattern—a pattern that results in wasting enormous amounts of money on sales and marketing strategies that were doomed to fail even before they were started.

Why were they doomed to fail? Because the people creating and executing them were never taught that there is a *process* to Sales and Marketing—a process that demands that you address each of the critical factors necessary to ensure success. Ignoring one or more of these factors will almost guarantee failure.

What? A *process* to Sales and Marketing? Oh no! Processes belong in Finance. They belong in Manufacturing. That's right, and they belong in Sales and Marketing too. This book is about applying some common sense business logic to the black magic of Sales and Marketing.

Before we venture into the how-to chapters of this book, it will help to understand what some of the most common problems are. As you read along about what's wrong with Marketing and Sales, think about your business and your experiences. Think about marketing and sales programs that succeeded and programs that failed, and see if *your* company practices these deadly sins.

WHO SHOULD READ THIS BOOK?

Business owners and CEOs should read this book for three reasons:

- First, it will help you decide how to structure your company, especially Marketing and Sales, for maximum efficiency.
- Second, it will heighten your awareness of how much of your spending in Sales and Marketing is invested wisely and how much is wasted.
- Third, it will make it easier for you to decide, based on sound business principles, where you should invest, and—sometimes more important—where you *shouldn't* invest your limited resources.

VPs of Sales should read this book because it provides a framework for changing your Sales organization from salespeople to skilled business managers—from people who run around making sales calls and putting out fires to people who can develop a business plan, execute it and manage it, at all times knowing where they are and what they have to do.

VPs of Marketing should read this book because it will change the way you market and it will change the way you motivate and manage the people in your organization. You may not reduce your marketing expenditures, but you will change the way you spend your money.

VPs of Sales and VPs of Marketing will also realize how dependent they are on each other's organizations and skills to be truly successful.

Hopefully, you will agree with our belief in the need to destroy the wall that exists between Sales and Marketing—and do something about it.

Salespeople should read this book because it will give you the skills that all the sales training programs neglect: the skills to run your territory like a business and to optimize the return on your investment.

Marketing personnel should read this book because it will change your outlook about what you do and how you do it. You will see how all of the pieces fit together and how important your role is to the ultimate success and profit of your company. Your role will shift from managing the things-to-do list to orchestrating a well-thought-out business plan.

Chief Financial Officers (CFOs) and Information Technology (IT) Managers should read this book because we need to stop managing Sales and Marketing with the "use it or lose it" budget mentality. We need to manage our investment in Sales and Marketing the way we manage other corporate investments, and you are critical to making that happen.

To all of the above, this book will give you the tough questions to ask.

CONTENT OF *THE BUCK STARTS HERE*

This book is written in three parts.

Part One—Danger Signs: The Most Common Mistakes Made in Sales and Marketing Today

Part One discusses some of the key symptoms—the danger signals—that tell you if your Sales and Marketing organizations might not be operating at peak efficiency. These danger signals are the ones we encounter most frequently in the many Sales and Marketing organizations we work with around the world.

Size is not a factor. Very small companies exhibit the same symptoms as large companies.

Success is not a factor. Companies that are very successful frequently have pockets of sales and marketing activities that are either misdirected or wasteful.

Money is not a factor, although having plenty of it allows you to do more. If you are doing more bad marketing, however, you are just burning money faster, because each misdirected marketing effort can cost months of delay, tens or hundreds of thousands of dollars of wasted time, money and effort and hundreds of thousands or millions in lost sales.

The critical factor is people—People who can combine common-sense business logic with the savvy, skill, creativity and art of sales and marketing.

We find that few people in Marketing and Sales actually have formal education or degrees in Marketing and Sales.

Salespeople come from all walks of life, and if they are very successful, their companies make them managers, usually without training them properly.

Many Marketing people are from Product Development or Engineering, because they know the product best. Other Marketing people may have degrees in Marketing or expertise in their chosen field, but they may lack the practical experience of selling and face-to-face customer contact, which makes it difficult for them to be truly effective.

Others who do Marketing are entrepreneurs, businesspeople, engineers—people who know they want to sell products but aren't sure how.

Most important, few people in Sales and Marketing understand how to read and interpret the profit-and-loss statements of their businesses. They are spending vast amounts of money without really understanding the impact on the bottom line.

Part Two—Methodology: The Road Map to Avoid Pitfalls

Part Two is the road map that shows you how to avoid the most common pitfalls. It will teach you how to develop, execute and manage sales and marketing strategies that make business sense. It discusses a practical, common sense, logical business approach to Sales and Marketing—an approach that anyone can use successfully even without extensive sales or marketing experience.

We are not suggesting that art and creativity aren't important to the success of your programs; they are vitally important. We are suggesting that the only reason you conduct sales and marketing is to accomplish some objective—ultimately to generate revenue *profitably*. If you fail to generate profit, then all the imagination and creativity in the world will not produce the dollars to allow you to stay in business.

By setting specific goals, you will learn where to begin, and how to move through the marketing process of identifying your target audience, understanding the Buy/Sell Cycle, choosing the best sales and marketing techniques, implementing and managing the process and, finally, learning how to evaluate what worked, what didn't work and why, so you can improve.

By using the process, you will learn what you know and what you don't know about your products, markets and competitors. You will identify the strengths and weaknesses of your strategy and you will find out if you can market your products and services profitably *before* you spend tens or hundreds of thousands of dollars on flawed sales and marketing programs.

You might even find out that you should *not* fund the development of a new product or enter a new market or get into that new business you are contemplating, because you can't do so profitably.

In order to put together a targeted, hard-hitting sales and marketing strategy, you must

- Establish your goals.
- Profile your target customer audience.
- Define what the customer must do in order to buy.
- Develop a sales and marketing strategy to make it happen.
- Execute the strategy.
- Manage your plan.
- Measure the results.

We focus on each of the foregoing items in the chapters that follow.

Epilogue—Where Are Sales and Marketing Going in the Future?

The Epilogue is a discussion about how Sales and Marketing must change to meet the demands of the future. It is based not only on our extensive experience but also on feedback from our clients.

It is a combination of opinion, speculation, guessing and common sense with the sole intention of getting you, the reader, to think about the future. We will give you insights into the following questions that you might be asking yourself.

- How will Sales and Marketing have to change to keep pace with changing markets and technology?
- How much will Sales and Marketing need to improve in efficiency to allow us to remain profitable and competitive five years from now?
- How will our competitors leverage their sales and marketing investments to establish a competitive edge over us?

IT'S A MATTER OF SURVIVAL . . . ANSWER THESE THREE KEY QUESTIONS

1. Can we continue to treat our sales and marketing budgets as an *expense* item, buried in SG&A (Sales, General and Administrative) on our balance sheet?
2. How do we manage our *investment* in Sales and Marketing as efficiently and effectively as we manage our investment in Manufacturing, in Distribution, in Engineering and in Product Development?
3. How much more money are we willing to burn on inefficient sales and marketing programs if we don't change?

A Word about Language . . .

Before we begin, a word about language. Our clients tell us that one of the intangible benefits they receive from *The Buck Starts Here* is the use of a common language—a language that everyone in the company—in Sales, Marketing, Engineering, Administration, Management, Finance— understands. Knowing how we use certain terminology throughout this book will help you get the most value from it. Here goes.

Customer

You probably have several words describing one's progression from suspect to prospect to qualified prospect to customer to repeat customer, and that is good. We tend to use the single word—customer— interchangeably with all of the above. It appears that when you think about prospects as happy customers, you care for them more, you expect them to become happy customers and as a result, they do.

Buying Cycle

The process you, and everyone else, go through when you buy something is the Buying Cycle. Your Buying Cycle may be very short (almost instantaneous) if you are buying something inexpensive or on a whim. The more expensive, complex or important the purchase, the longer and more difficult the Buying Cycle. In both cases, the processes of buying are remarkably alike.

Sales Cycle

The various techniques you use to get people to buy constitute the Sales Cycle. Frequently, people spend so much time thinking how they are going to *sell* something to someone that they ignore or forget the customer's Buying Cycle. The unfortunate result can be lots of sales and marketing *activities* but not enough sales.

Business Goal

Usually, the business goal translates into revenue and profit and the number of customers who need to buy. We encourage everyone to set specific, challenging, attainable business goals each and every time you use *The Buck Starts Here.*

Sometimes valid business goals do not translate easily to revenue and profit—such as corporate image and branding campaigns—but you must still treat them as investments, track the results and understand the return on investment based on those results.

Burning Money

Burning money means wasting money, throwing it away. You burn money when you produce a fancy, eight-color executive brochure that nobody reads. You burn money when you attract people to your booth at a trade show by offering two free tickets to Bermuda and then treating everyone who drops a business card into the fishbowl as if they were real prospects.

There are lots of very creative ways to burn money in sales and marketing. If you are not tracking the results of your sales and marketing expenditures, you are most likely burning money.

If you *want* to burn money in sales and marketing, why waste your time and resources? Give it to us. We'll burn it for you—without charge.

Return on Investment (ROI)

You can use ROI or any other expression that gets to the real point: can you sell your product profitably? We have seen sales and marketing plans whose total cost of sales and marketing exceeded the revenue projected—obviously not a good way to stay in business. If you can't identify the return on your sales and marketing investment, you are burning money.

Examples of the various ways you can look at the return on your sales and marketing investment are in Part Two, Chapter 7 ("Matching Your Sales Cycle to the Customer's Buying Cycle") and Chapter 9 ("Creating Hard-Hitting and On-Target Sales and Marketing Strategies").

. . . and Punctuation

We have chosen to capitalize terms such as Buying Cycle, Sales Cycle, Sales, Marketing, and others in order to provide emphasis and clarity. Our apologies to English purists who might choose the use of lower case.

WHAT YOU CAN EXPECT FROM *THE BUCK STARTS HERE*

In this book, we will provide you with tools to do the following.

- Establish realistic, attainable business goals.
- Profile your target customer audience.
- Focus on the actions that lead to sales and satisfied customers.
- Define the results you want from your sales and marketing effort.
- Choose the best vehicles for delivering your messages.
- Collect and analyze sales and marketing data to measure results.
- Build strong teamwork between Marketing, Sales, Engineering, Manufacturing and Finance.
- Determine resource constraints and alternative channels of distribution.
- Determine the cost of executing your sales and marketing strategy and compare it with the revenue expected.

WHOM SHOULD YOU INVOLVE IN ROI-BASED SALES AND MARKETING?

ROI-based Sales and Marketing is both a thought process and a way of creating, implementing and measuring hard-hitting, customer-focused sales and marketing plans. Because this thought process puts the customer first and foremost, it may require changes in your company. These changes may have to be in:

- How you currently create sales and marketing plans
- How (or whether) you measure sales and marketing results
- How you evaluate/measure the performance of Marketing and Sales organizations

The best people to create, implement and measure your sales and marketing plans are those who are responsible for them. It is best to work with cross-functional teams to create plans. The following departments should be represented on the team of 10–15 people.

- Marketing (4 or 5 people with 1 very strong individual to act as the team captain)
- Sales (2 or 3)
- Engineering (1 or 2)
- Service (1 or 2)
- Manufacturing (1)
- Finance (1)

Depending on the size of your company, you might want to keep the teams to 4 or 5 people. Just make sure that you've assembled the team on a cross-functional basis with Marketing and Sales represented (mandatory) and other departments as needed (optional—depends on your company's needs).

In order for this process to work most efficiently, it must be:

- Driven from the top down—not the bottom up—in your organization
- Committed to by senior-level management
- Pervasive in all aspects of Marketing and Sales: from planning to action to measurement to analysis

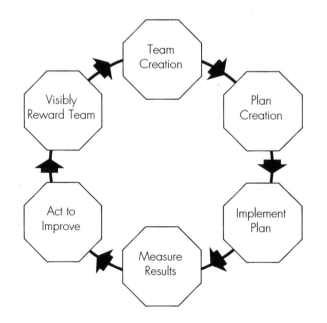

DANGER SIGNS: THE MOST COMMON MISTAKES MADE in SALES AND MARKETING TODAY

Part One consists of:

- Chapter 1: The Challenges Faced in Sales and Marketing Today
- Chapter 2: Danger Signs: The Most Common Mistakes Made in Sales and Marketing Today
- Chapter 3: ROI-Based Sales and Marketing: The Process and How It Works

Chapter 1 focuses on questions that ask you to think about your own company. What kind of behavior are you reinforcing in your own Sales and Marketing organizations?

Chapter 2 looks at the ten deadly sins of Sales and Marketing. It in we'll ask you to make an honest assessment of your own company.

Chapter 3 introduces ROI-Based Sales and Marketing, which is a process that can help you determine the actual cost of selling and marketing a product as well as the projected revenue before you spend any money on Sales and Marketing. We have implemented ROI-Based Sales and Marketing in hundreds of companies with amazing results. One major company identified that it could have saved $500,000 in just one marketing initiative if it had used these techniques.

The Challenges Faced in Sales and Marketing Today

I

Sales and Marketing organizations today are facing a major challenge. The Management of their companies is expecting outstanding results. Competition is getting tougher and tougher. Marketing, combined with Sales, is being asked to lead the charge.

Quite often sales and marketing people find themselves facing a dilemma. They are working within a 20-year-old sales model (let's do this, let's do that, let's say this, let's say that, and in the end the customer will buy), but they are finding that the model is outmoded and outdated. Customers aren't necessarily buying, and when they do, Sales and Marketing don't know exactly why.

Corporate executives may be asking the right questions,

- Are we spending too much/too little on sales and marketing?
- What impact is our sales and marketing investment having on our revenue?
- How do we attract new customers?
- How do we introduce new products?
- What's working, what's not working, and why?
- How should we sell our products—through sales calls, direct mail, telemarketing, alternate channels of distribution—and why will one vehicle work better than another?
- How much will our sales and marketing strategy cost, and how does that compare with the revenue we expect?
- How can we change our sales and marketing strategy to improve our return on investment (ROI)?

but those executives' Marketing and Sales organizations may not have the proper tools, motivation or internal corporate culture to get the best answers.

This book, *The Buck Starts Here*, is aimed at answering those and many other questions. ROI-based Sales and Marketing is an innovative methodology that will help you get the most from your sales and marketing investments. The book offers you the tools you need to evaluate the effectiveness of your current sales and marketing programs, and the ROI-based Sales and Marketing methodology offers solutions to your sales and marketing challenges that work in the real world.

The premise of this book is that sales and marketing should be run like a business. With any business, you make investments and expect a return on investment from them. So too with sales and marketing. You should expect a measurable, tangible return on investment from your sales and marketing expenditures, and we will show you how. *The Buck Starts Here* contains a practical, common sense approach to sales and marketing. You do not need to be a marketing professional, nor do you need a marketing degree to gain great results from this book. If you are a marketing professional or you have a marketing degree, *The Buck Starts Here* is unlike any marketing methodology you have seen to date. We will focus on the business of sales and marketing and on your return on investment from it.

WHAT'S THE DIFFERENCE BETWEEN SALES AND MARKETING?

When we ask this question in our workshops, the answers are generally along the following lines.

- Sales is what the "Sales" organization does—the personal contact with customers—getting the order—managing the customer relationship—"you know: 'sales.'"
- Marketing is "broader." It's market research and product definition; it's advertising and marketing conditioning; it's "supporting" Sales— "you know: 'Marketing.'"

Then we ask the "suppose" questions.

- Suppose a salesperson in the field sends out 20 letters a week to generate leads in his or her territory. Is that sales or is it marketing?
- Suppose someone in marketing back at headquarters contacts prospects by phone and sells them products. It that sales or is it marketing?
- Suppose you sell products through advertising. It that sales or is it marketing?
- Suppose you sell products through a mail piece. It that sales or is it marketing?

Is Sales part of Marketing or is Marketing part of Sales?

The dictionary definitions of Sales and Marketing are not important. What is important is that companies create different structures—the Sales Department and the Marketing Department. This forced separation creates an environment that fosters lack of communication and cooperation; turf wars abound and predominate.

The only reason we sell or market is to get people to do something—usually, to buy our products or services. To accomplish this in increasingly competitive markets, Sales and Marketing can't be operating at less than 100% efficiency; they need to integrate their activities and complement each other.

We encourage the use of selling teams to develop and manage the execution of key sales and marketing strategies. Such selling teams consist of cross-functional participants—sales, communications, advertising, product development, engineering, finance, customer service, and so on. The mission of the team is to ensure that attainable, executable *and profitable* sales and marketing strategies are put in place and managed.

If the selling team is unable to develop a profitable business case, don't shoot the messenger. You are better off knowing the obstacles now instead of six months or two years from now.

If you can't sell a product profitably, why develop it?

DOES THIS SOUND LIKE YOUR COMPANY OR ORGANIZATION?

To many people, marketing is abstract, artistic and difficult to define. When sales are not up to expectation, the reaction is to throw more money at it or do it differently. How many of the following statements describe you—or your organization?

- You know you should be selling more, but you're not sure why you aren't.
- Your Sales and Marketing groups do not work together, or they are frequently at odds with each other about sales and marketing strategies.
- You spend a lot of money on marketing activities, but don't really know what to expect or how to track results.
- You allocate a marketing budget—which is on the increase—instead of managing marketing on an ROI basis. How much should we *invest* in this marketing program, and what *results* should we expect from that investment?
- Your Sales and Marketing groups are still using the old model of selling instead of changing sales and marketing strategies to meet the new, competitive market conditions.
- You are announcing new products or entering new markets and don't know what to expect.

If one or more of these statements depict you, then you need *The Buck Starts Here.*

REALITIES OF MARKETING TODAY

How Marketing Budgets Are Determined

In many companies, the marketing "spend" budget is determined by multiplying the expected revenue of the organization or product times the company's designated marketing spend percentage. The spend percentage amount for marketing can vary from 1 or 2% to 20% or more (depending on the business and its needs). So, for example, if the projected revenue for a product is $2 million and the marketing spend percentage for the company is 2%, then the marketing budget would be $40,000. The obvious question is, "Is $40,000 too little, enough or too much to spend on marketing this product?" Most companies have no idea.

In many other cases, it is by no means that scientific. Marketing budgets are arrived at by:

- the political, internal factors driving a particular product or service
- plain old gut feel
- whoever does the best sales job

Many factors drive what the marketing spend budget should be for a particular product or service. Many things should be taken into consideration, such as:

- the projected revenue *and* profit
- whether the product is a new one or is an established one (such as a cash cow)
- what the channels of distribution are (i.e., how the product is sold to the end consumer)
- whether the need for this particular product is well-known or whether the company has to actually establish the market

How do you *know* how much should be spent to market a particular product or service?

The methodology described in the following chapters will discuss how you determine this.

How Marketing Is Measured

If we were to examine the various functions within a company, most of the departments can be asked certain bottom-line questions to determine their success.

Sales can be asked, "How many did you sell? What was the revenue? What was the profit?"

Engineering can be asked, "Were the products that you engineered designed on time? On budget?"

Finance can be asked, "Did you save money? Cut costs? By how much?"

Manufacturing can be asked "Was the manufacturing process completed as swiftly and efficiently as possible? What is the downtime for any particular piece of equipment? Is just the right amount of inventory available at all times so that the manufacturing process has no delays?"

Distribution/Logistics can be asked, "Were all orders picked within 24 hours of order placement? How many inventory turns do we have? What is our shrinkage rate?"

Research can be asked, "How many of your ideas have become products?"

Service delivery can be asked, "What is your revenue? What is your customer satisfaction ratio?"

And, finally, Marketing can be asked, "How much revenue did you deliver? How many activities did you do?"

BEHAVIOR DRIVEN WITHIN MARKETING ORGANIZATIONS TODAY

The two questions, How much revenue did you deliver? and How many activities did you do? drive an incredible amount of spending and activity within marketing organizations today.

Let's examine both questions:

How much revenue did you deliver?

Can Marketing really be measured solely on the delivery of revenue? How many marketing programs really generate revenue?

Do trade shows and other events? Yes, if orders are taken directly on the floor. If orders are not taken directly on the floor, the attainment of revenue from the event can be misleading. What really contributed to that order, and how can we attribute the order solely to the event? We have seen situations where companies have attributed revenue directly to an event, and yet the sales force had been working with that customer for three years prior to the event and the customer decided to buy at the event. Does the event rightly deserve the "buy" credit?

Does direct mail? Yes, if you are receiving orders through the mail, as in a catalog sale. If revenue does not come directly from the mail piece, then it is very hard to measure the piece on the revenue generated.

How about telemarketing? It's the same thing as direct mail. If you are selling something over the phone and an order comes in, then by all means, attribute the order to that vehicle. But if you are telemarketing to generate awareness or to get a customer to move up the buy cycle (e.g., to attend a seminar to gain in-depth information), then you cannot measure that vehicle solely on revenue.

The point here is that you can't measure a marketing activity solely on revenue unless you can measure or prove that the revenue is a direct result of this activity.

How many activities did you do?

This question more than any other drives a frenetic pace within Marketing today. People are valued on their activities more so than their content or their results.

If John is a marketing person and completes 20 activities, and Jane is in the same group and has the same job and completes 25, who is perceived as the better marketeer? Jane, of course.

The right answer is, It depends. And it truly does. Our contention is that the value of the marketing person is not in doing a lot of stuff. The value is in whether or not the person has moved the customer forward in the customer's buy cycle. In Chapter 6 we'll talk more about moving customers forward in their Buying Cycle.

When people focus on activities, here's what they do.

- They focus on internal activities.
- They make decisions in a vacuum, rushing from one activity to the next.
- They know when an activity is completed but not necessarily the result of it.

- They don't know what worked and what didn't, because they do not measure what happened as a result of the marketing activity.
- They do not know how to improve.
- They manage their to-do list instead of managing their business.

We call this frenetic activities-based marketing approach the Alice-in-Wonderland-and-the-Red-Queen syndrome. Remember when Alice was running in a circle with the Red Queen? She was running as fast as she could but was not going anywhere, and the Red Queen said, "Now! Now! Faster! Faster!" That's what it's like to market without a plan; that's what it's like to market purely for activities' sake. Marketing people rush from one marketing activity to the next. They never know what the real result of the activity was—just that they did it and they will do more. They work fast and furiously but are never really sure what they just accomplished.

Many times, Sales makes the comment, "Those Marketing people really don't know our customers. They really don't understand what's going on out here."

THE ALTERNATIVES

Here are our choices: We can measure Marketing purely on revenue (which we have seen is not always a good measure, particularly if a lot of our marketing activities are aimed at customer awareness). We can measure Marketing on activities—and that's what we'll get: a lot of activities.

Or, we can measure Marketing on moving the customer forward in the Buying Cycle.

WHAT'S THE CUSTOMER'S BUYING CYCLE?

I'm sure you've heard of the Sales Cycle. That's what most people talk about. The Sales Cycle consists of the activities that you do to get the customer to buy.

Here's the catch. If we focus on the Sales Cycle first, we are being very egocentric—me, me, me. I'm going to do this; then I'll do that, then the other thing and then the customer will buy. Right? Wrong. The customer does not always buy.

Don't we have it backwards? First we need to focus on the customers—who they are, where they are, what's important to them, what they must do in order to buy our product or service. Once we focus on the customers and the customers' Buying Cycle, we can then match our Sales Cycle to their Buying Cycle so that we can help them move through their Buying Cycle as quickly and efficiently as possible.

The customer and the customer's Buying Cycle come first. Our Sales Cycle (what we will say, do and measure) comes second. When both are added together with fine-tuning adjustments to make ourselves more efficient, we have an ROI-based sales and marketing strategy.

2

Danger Signs: The Most Common Mistakes Made in Sales and Marketing Today

As we mentioned in the beginning of this book, we have trained more than 3,000 Sales, Marketing and Businesspeople worldwide. Therefore, we have had the opportunity to examine and dissect many sales and marketing strategies and programs. In this chapter, we will focus on what we call "The Ten Deadly Sins of Sales and Marketing." These are the things that we have seen companies do that are consistently wrong. These sins cause more spending than is necessary and even revenue loss. However, we won't leave it at that. The rest of the book will focus on the right things to do in sales and marketing—those things that will manage the cost of Sales and Marketing and focus on driving increased *revenue* and *profit*.

"I DON'T DO SALES; I'M IN MARKETING."

The first deadly sin in Sales and Marketing is the way some companies are organized.

The Sales organization generally consists of salespeople and sales managers. They probably have quotas, get paid commissions and *always* know if they are ahead of, on, or behind plan. Salespeople who consistently miss quota usually find new careers.

The Marketing organization generally consists of people who do marketing—people with expertise in market research, advertising, communications, event coordination, brochure production, and so on. They are people who know how to put together a marketing plan that ensures that "all the bases are touched" so as to guarantee success in the marketplace.

In many cases, this stovepipe type of organization leads to significant inefficiencies, frequently caused by lack of communication between Sales (the selling organization) and Marketing (the marketing organization).

When you delve under the covers, this should be no surprise to you. The reality is that many Sales and Marketing organizations have different business objectives and are managed differently.

The most obvious differences between these organizations is the measurement system used to define success. In Sales, this measurement system is based on some form of quota. If Sales exceeds quota, they are stars and are well compensated and rewarded. If they fail to achieve quota, they look for another career. Since quotas tend to be clearly defined, such as the number of units or amount of revenue, measuring success is easy. Sales might have an expense budget relative to its revenue objectives, but little attention is paid to whether Sales is selling efficiently and *profitably*.

Marketing, on the other hand, does not typically have specific, stated business goals. In most organizations, Marketing has a budget, usually negotiated based on last year's budget and incremented by next year's resources and product projections. The marketing plan is a detailed list of *spending* activities: ad campaigns, trade shows, four-color executive brochures, sales training, and so forth. It is difficult to measure Marketing's impact on Sales, so if Sales achieves its objectives, obviously Marketing did a good job. Right? If Sales *doesn't* make the objectives, whose fault was it?

Marketing organizations that are funded on a use-it-or-lose-it budget basis are usually very activities focused, where the people who do more marketing activities are considered the better people.

Think about a spend-the-budget-type of motivation. Do you really want to motivate your Marketing organization to spend its time fig-

Do you wonder why we include the phrase "from you" when we say something like ". . . easier for your customer to buy from you?" Some of our clients have learned that their awareness/image/education-type campaigns do accomplish part of their objective: they are effective in educating a market and in creating demand for products. The problem, however, is that poorly crafted sales messages that do not differentiate *your* products and that you can create just as much demand for your *competition* as for your own products. Would you like to condition the market for your competitors? Would you like to let them reap the rewards of your work because they *have* differentiated their products and services from everyone else's?

It's not enough to create demand for a product. You must focus on getting customers to buy—from you.

uring out how to *spend* your money (the marketing plan) and then being managed to spend that money? The result of this kind of thinking will be lots of activity but not necessarily lots of sales.

This book is about a different way to organize your Sales and Marketing organizations into effective, integrated selling teams focused not on spending money but on *investing* your resources—people, time, money—in the best selling strategies to get your customer to buy—from *you*.

"WE HAVE TO MAKE SOME BIG NUMBERS. LET'S ADVERTISE!"

The second deadly sin is the failure to define specific business goals. Now, we all know that management is good at defining the *size* of the revenue increase we need next year to achieve our growth objective, but management is poor at defining *where* that business is coming from.

- How much is coming from existing customers?
- New customers?

- Competitive penetration?
- Large accounts?
- Small accounts?
- In what geographies?

Failure to specify the niches of customers to which you must successfully market to achieve your total revenue objective leads to a number of bad investments in Sales and Marketing.

In some cases, the revenue objective is so big that it is difficult to comprehend and is frightening to people. When you have millions or billions of dollars in sales to generate, Marketing tends to gravitate toward broad-based marketing strategies, advertising campaigns that will create "market pull," "awareness" campaigns and other ways to consume large amounts of money on difficult-to-measure marketing activities with murky (if any) business objectives.

The problem with these types of campaigns is not just that they are difficult to manage or measure; they also tend to use watered-down sales messages that are so general that they don't convince anybody to do anything.

On the Sales side, these huge quotas cause more hiring to put the "feet in the street" to achieve the objectives. But are Salespeople necessarily the best way to get the customer to buy? Are they the best channel of distribution? What is the return on investment from Sales' involvement? Without an analysis of where the business is coming from, you'll never know. You'll just hire and hope for the best.

Another danger is that Management is focused so much on growing the business that they lose sight of the bottom line: *profit*. If the focus is on growth, make sure you can do it profitably.

The Buck Starts Here shows how you can and must set business goals that are definable, manageable and attainable so that everyone in your selling organization knows exactly what their business objectives are—from the salesperson on the street to the communications person developing your brochures and from the Vice Presidents of Sales, Marketing and Finance to the CEO.

"My market is the Fortune 500."

The third deadly sin is that companies don't know their customers. "Baloney," you say. "We know our customers." Well, you might, and that is goodness.

The harsh reality is that many companies really do not know who their customers are, why the customers buy or how they buy.

The most common cause of this problem is organizational: Marketing supports the sales force, creates demand and does a lot of activities. In this type of organization, Marketing rarely talks to real, live customers because that's considered the job of Sales. Besides, they don't have *time* to talk to customers; they have to get that brochure out or get ready for that trade show.

The marketing staff in this type of organization has little or no selling experience and in some cases, little marketing experience. Because they might have come to Marketing from Engineering or Product Development, they were deemed to know the product best but were not trained on how to market powerfully and effectively or how to understand their customers and why or how customers buy. The net result is that they do a lot of activities and consider this the value added of Marketing.

Sometimes, lack of knowledge about customers is caused by the channel of distribution utilized in a company. If you sell to the end user—the consumer of your product—through some channel, be it a wholesaler, retailer, reseller, value-added remarketer or even your own sales force, your awareness and knowledge of your customers will be distorted by the channel. In some cases, the channel will try to prevent your access to your own customer.

If you don't think this is a problem in your company, try a little test. Choose 10 salespeople who recently made sales to 10 customers. Ask the salespeople why the customers bought. Then ask the customers. You might be surprised. We were.

Another problem is that those in Marketing are so busy doing activities and supporting Sales that they think that *Sales* is their customer, because if Marketing can't get Sales to push the product, Marketing will miss the plan.

The last time we checked, Sales was a vehicle through which you sold your products. Sales *sells* your products; it doesn't buy them. The *customer* buys your products and gives you money for them. Don't confuse the two. Sales is a channel of distribution, as are resellers, other equipment manufacturers, telemarketing, direct mail catalogs, and so on.

When we ask, Who is your customer? during our workshops, people frequently say their customer is some market segment like the Fortune 500 or large manufacturing companies. But the Fortune 500 have never bought anything. *People* buy from you, and the better you know who they are and why they buy, the more successful you will be.

"WHO CARES ABOUT BUYING? ALL I WANT TO DO IS SELL, SELL, SELL."

The fourth deadly sin is not knowing your customer's Buying Cycle, which should be no surprise if you don't know your customers very well.

Think about the way you yourself buy things. Your buying process probably begins when you realize that you want or need something. After that, you might do some basic fact finding about what is available and how much it might cost.

If you are still interested, you might do some more in-depth research and even compare several vendors' products. Along the way, you might seek the advice of friends, experts or business associates. At this point, you will probably decide whether you have the money and want to spend it on the product. Then you buy and use the product and sometimes buy more.

You go through this type of process every time you buy something. If you see something you like in a store or catalog, the entire process from awareness to executing the buy decision might take seconds.

Buying a new car or house takes longer and is usually more complex.

Buying a new computer system might take months and involve hundreds of people.

If you don't know how your customer buys—the buying process—then how can you develop an efficient, successful selling strategy? Your selling strategy should be designed to move your customers through their buying cycle as quickly and easily as possible, and you can do that only if you know how and why your customers buy.

In complex buying scenarios, you might have several buyers, each with their own cycle. You might have decision makers, technical evaluators, recommenders, champions, approvers or advisers. Ignoring the needs of any key player will probably cost you the sale. Even selling a car might involve several buyers and several Buy Cycles, with a husband, a wife and children playing different roles in the process.

If Sales doesn't know the Buying Cycle, they will frequently lose business because they didn't know that a key person was involved or a critical step needed to be taken. However, your competition may have done their homework—and may have gotten the order.

When Marketing isn't thinking about how to move a customer through the Buying Cycle, they tend to spend most, or all, of its time, money and resources at the beginning of the Buying Cycle—the awareness stage—and spend little or no resources moving the customer *through* the cycle to the buy/implement decision. This is frequently the case when Marketing does marketing and Sales does selling.

Sales *is* marketing. Marketing *is* selling.

Perhaps all Sales and Marketing departments should be replaced by *Selling* departments.

If you know your customers—how they buy and why they buy—you can develop an efficient selling strategy that makes it easier for your customers to buy—from you.

"MY THING IS FASTER THAN YOUR THING—AND BIGGER TOO. WOW!"

The fifth deadly sin consists of poorly crafted sales messages.

Take a good hard look at your sales messages and those of your competitors. Evaluate how powerful your messages are. Are they powerful enough to get the targeted audience to take action? To change its beliefs? To move through the Buying Cycle?

YOU CAN'T SKIP THE HARD PART OF SALES MESSAGES

The hard part of sales messages is understanding and then telling your prospects *how your product will benefit them.*

Creating powerful sales messages that your customers understand and believe is hard work, perhaps the most difficult part of marketing. Most companies focus on the easy part of sales messages, the "me" part—the lists of features that our product has (we're bigger, faster, greener, quieter and cheaper) and that's where they stop.

Consider how weak a features-type sales message is.

Say that your ads claim your products are "faster," "will increase your productivity" and "last longer." What is your competition saying? That its product is slower, will decrease customers' productivity and won't last long? Of course not. You are all saying the same things. So how can prospects differentiate your product from others? It's not making it easier to buy from you; it makes it harder to buy.

Powerful sales messages are written in the *customer's* language—not yours. They address the emotional and business needs of customers by discussing the benefits and impact on the customer and/or the customer's business. Good sales messages translate how your product benefits the customer, so customers don't have to figure it out for themselves. Good sales messages are believable and quantify whenever possible. Good messages address "what keeps your customer awake at night."

Poor sales messages affect not only sales but also the sales productivity of your Sales organization, especially in larger, more complex sales in which the decision maker is the president or senior manager of a company. We have found that three out of four salespeople selling in a complex partnership type of selling environment know who the decision maker is, but are not calling on the decision maker regularly.

Why? Because the salespeople can't talk in the CEO's language about things that keep the CEO awake at night. The CEO doesn't want to hear the platitudes about faster, cheaper, and so forth. The CEO wants to get to the bottom line—to learn how your product is going to increase sales, reduce costs, make the CEO's company more competitive.

Case in point: During a workshop, we asked a client, Why should your customer buy that from you? and the response after much discussion was "Because it will increase the customer's productivity." "How much?" we asked. "We don't know," was the answer.

With more work, we were able to define *how much* the product could increase productivity, *who* would be affected, and *the potential impact* on the business. In the case we just described, the *who* that would benefit were salespeople who used the product to do their jobs faster; the *how much* was 30 minutes per sales rep per day in time savings, and the *potential impact* on the business was the equivalent of $24 million per year for a sales force of over 5,000 people.

Now, what type of sales calls are your salespeople making? Do they stop at "improve productivity," or can they explain how your product can impact productivity, why that should be important to the customer, and how much impact it will have on the business?

Are they talking about improved productivity or $24 million?

Powerful sales messages can make it easier for your customers to buy—from you. The impact on your business will be increased sales, lower sales costs and happier customers.

"WHAT WE NEED IS A VIDEOTAPE."

The sixth deadly sin is developing sales and marketing plans that "have the appropriate mix of marketing and communications vehicles to ensure broad-based penetration in our target markets" or some such marketspeak.

All that means is that the budget will be spent (efficiently, of course) on everything you can imagine—from sales calls to trade shows, from brochures to infomercials, focus groups and Super Bowl ads—to ensure that "all the bases have been touched." That way, if the plan isn't achieved, no one can blame marketing for not doing something. And, in fact, marketing really doesn't know if one vehicle is better than another; therefore, they do it all. Some people call this approach, "spray-and-pray" marketing; you spray the money around and then you pray that you will achieve the results.

We have seen marketing programs that had so many activities that the cost of the marketing programs *exceeded the revenue* expected, because people focused on marketing activities instead of results.

How does this happen? When Marketing and Sales are stovepiped, Marketing usually does market-awareness-and-support-type activities and Sales does sales-type activities. Marketing spends its budget. Sales spends its budget as well. In that type of stovepiped organization, no one adds up the total cost of Sales and Marketing. No one is looking at the Buying Cycle of the customer to determine who should do what and when it should be done to move customers through the Buying Cycle.

The result is that Marketing does "awareness-and-lead-generation" campaigns and Sales does "prospecting." Not only do these overlapping activities waste lots of money, but also they frequently result in the target customer audience's getting different sales messages from Marketing and Sales.

This book will show how to determine which sales and marketing activities to use at each stage of the Buying Cycle. It will focus on moving people through the Buying Cycle with an integrated sales and marketing strategy that can be tracked and managed. It will provide tools to help you to understand your sales and marketing costs and the return on investment for each and every stage of the customer's Buying Cycle.

IF YOU'RE NOT KEEPING SCORE, HOW DO YOU KNOW IF YOU'RE SUCCEEDING OR FAILING?

The seventh deadly sin is Management demanding and rewarding sales and marketing *activities* instead of rewarding people for the *results* they get. If a sales rep's sales are down, Management wants the rep to make more calls. So too, with Marketing: when sales are down, we need to do more marketing or a better marketing job.

Well, making more *bad* sales calls will not improve results. Doing more *bad* marketing will not improve results either. To improve results, we need to know what is happening and why it is happening. We need to keep score. Then we have a chance of improving.

Now, keeping score is pretty easy if you are in Manufacturing, Finance or Distribution. In fact, you probably couldn't run your company if you didn't know exactly what inventory was in stock or exactly what your accounts receivable are. You know exactly how much it costs to build your product and how much it costs to deliver it. Before investing in a new manufacturing, engineering or distribution facility, you need to know all of the costs; the expected production; the exact improvements in quality, efficiency and costs; and the impact it will have on the bottom line.

Why then, do so few people know how much it costs to make a sale?

Why is it that practically every aspect of running your business is saturated with information technology solutions, except sales and marketing?

Why is it that we have integrated manufacturing systems, integrated financial systems, integrated logistics systems and integrated integrated systems, and *maybe* sales and marketing has some limited-function, lead-tracking, word-processing system.

Sales and Marketing is the orphan of information technology, and the time has come to change. Sales and Marketing is one of the largest line items on your financial statements—sometimes *the* largest—and many companies still bury it in SG&A (Sales, General and Administrative).

Companies that have implemented just-in-time inventory systems to reduce cost and increase efficiency and quality continue to spend millions of dollars on marketing programs without knowing either what results to expect or what results they do get, because the information system needed to track the sales and marketing *process* is not in place.

This book describes the manufacturing process of a sale. It provides the logic and the tools that show how to mold raw materials—prospects—into finished products—happy customers.

It gives you the tools that describe the resources you need to build your products and when to use them. When the process is used properly, you will know exactly who has to do something that needs to be done, when and how much it will cost. The book provides the basic logic for an integrated information technology solution for Sales and Marketing.

By using the tools and techniques in this book, Sales and Marketing can begin to implement basic measurement and management techniques that will help improve the sales and marketing process, but information technology tools are needed to do this properly. Without these tools, it is extremely difficult for Sales and Marketing to measure the results of what they do, and—

> IF YOU'RE NOT GOING TO
> MEASURE THE RESULTS, DON'T BOTHER
> DOING THE ACTIVITY. YOU WON'T KNOW IF
> YOU'RE SUCCESSFUL OR NOT.
> IN SHORT, YOU ARE BURNING MONEY.

"I'M GLAD THAT'S OVER. LET'S DO IT AGAIN!"

The eighth deadly sin is ending the sales and marketing process before it is over.

The job isn't over when we get the order—or lose it.

The job isn't over when we leave the trade show on the last day, exhausted.

The job isn't over when we ship the brochure to the printer. Neither is it over once the 10,000 (or 50,000) direct mail letters go to the post office.

The job isn't over until we know the results we got, understand what worked and what didn't work, know why we got the results we did and how we could improve so that we can do better the next time.

The process—the art of sales and marketing—is not right and wrong. It is a process of continuous improvement. Test, measure, evaluate and improve.

Companies that don't track what's working (or not working) and why tend to have knee jerk reactions, resulting in poor sales and marketing investments. One company that got poor response from a direct mail piece immediately rented another list and sent out the same letter, because it needed more leads. The list was not the problem at all. By talking to some people who received the mailing, we found out that the problem was in the sales messages, which were not convincing enough to get people to act. By improving the sales messages, the original list produced excellent results.

The reason people didn't come to your seminar might be that the mailbag is still in the post office.

Sales may not be getting orders because the sales messages are weak or too complex. Perhaps a sales tool is needed to increase the success rate.

You must track the results in order to know what is happening.

When you find out what works, do more of it. When you find out what doesn't work, try to improve the process.

"WE'RE ANNOUNCING OUR NEW PRODUCT NEXT WEEK. DID ANYONE TELL MARKETING AND SALES?"

The ninth deadly sin is that Marketing and Sales get involved in the product development process too late to have any significant impact. Sometimes, Sales never gets on board.

Why? Because companies routinely invest hundreds of thousands or millions of dollars in Product Development, Engineering and Manufacturing before Marketing is involved. Sure, Marketing may be informed, but it is too busy (with spending the budget on activities) to really get involved.

Shortly before the product announcement, panic sets in. Drop everything! Marketing has to put together a "launch plan" that ensures a successful rollout to the sales force. "Let's see: Let's do some advertising . . . We need a brochure—four-color enough? . . . Specification sheets are a must . . . Oops, can't forget the big trade show. Do we have time to get in? . . . What kind of training will we do for Sales? Will they come?

When the product's sales fail to meet expectations six months later, what happens? Obviously, the rollout wasn't as successful as it should have been. As Marketing reminds Management, "Remember those budget cuts? We told you we needed more money to create some *real* pull!" If we're going to bail this product out, we're going to have to do some *real* marketing. Let's force the salespeople to get in here and get product training. Let's relaunch with a direct mail campaign, coordinated with some great ads." Let's, let's, let's—*spend more money!*

Does any of this sound familiar? Are we exaggerating? We suggest that we are not. We have seen this scenario dozens of times. So, if this sounds familiar to you, stop the spiral!

Sales and Marketing should be working with Product Development *before* you make significant funding decisions, not after you spent the money. The best Sales and Marketing organizations can't save a bad product or even a good product that is positioned and priced incorrectly.

Before funding, develop the sales and marketing plan for the product. In other words, develop the selling plan. Define your target market; profile your customers; understand their buying cycle (we'll get into this in great detail in Part Two, Chapter 6); begin to develop the sales messages (Why should people buy this product? and why from you?); understand your competitive positioning at the time of announcement and afterward, not just now.

Most important, define how you will sell the product, and calculate your cost of Sales and Marketing to determine if you can sell it *profitably.*

You won't be able to answer all of the questions that early in the product development cycle, but you will find out what you do and don't know about the product, the competition, the available markets, customers, and so on.

If there's something you don't know and it is critical for your success, you have time to do the research to get the answers, improving the quality of your decisions. If you develop a selling plan *after* the product is in development and almost out the door, you will not have any time to:

- Change the product (as the market, competition and customer demands change)
- Change the sales messages (what you think customers want, need and value, they may not; your assumptions might be incorrect)
- Change the launch plan

Continue the process of Sales and Marketing involvement throughout development, reacting to market conditions, technology and improvements in your selling process. Each step on the way, ask tough questions, such as:

- How much should we spend to develop this product if it will not be superior to the competition's at announcement?
- Should we continue development if we can't describe how our customers will benefit from it? Why they buy it? How they buy it? What sales messages will motivate them to buy it?

Your decision to proceed or to stop should be based on the quality of the answers to questions such as these, with participation from Product Development, Engineering, Finance, Manufacturing *and* Sales and Marketing.

The key question is, Can we market and sell this product profitably? If the answer is yes, proceed. If the answer is no, what valid business reason exists that dictates continued investment in this product?

WHAT? ME? WORRY?

The tenth deadly sin is ignoring any of the first nine. People know that there are problems that must be addressed, and yet they just go on their merry way. They refuse to change, and they refuse to get others to change. They constantly refer to Management buy-in. They refuse to see that they are empowered: just simply assume the responsibility, stand up to the challenge and move forward.

Trying to sell in tomorrow's competitive environment by using techniques that were successful 10 and 20 years ago but are not today will put you out of business.

The tenth deadly sin is complacency.

ROI-Based Sales and Marketing: The Process and How It Works

3

We've just spent an entire chapter discussing what's wrong with Sales and Marketing.* So, now you've got to be asking yourself, "OK, now that I know what's wrong, how do I sell and market correctly? How can I *ensure* my success?" If you always ask yourself the following six questions, you will be successful in executing ROI-based Sales and Marketing.

SIX KEY QUESTIONS

1. Whom do you want to take action?
2. What do you want them to do?
3. What will you say to them to persuade them to take the action?
4. What will you do to get them to take the action?
5. How will you know if they have done it?
6. How will you measure it?

As we step through the methodology, we will refer back to these steps. You can identify the steps by looking for:

≈≋ STEP # _____ ≋≈

Each of these components is like a piece of a puzzle. If we do not have each piece, we will not have a complete picture. Likewise, as we

---

*We have provided a Sales and Marketing Self-Health Test on page 234 in the Appendix. This test will help you to determine the strengths and weaknesses of your Sales and Marketing organizations.

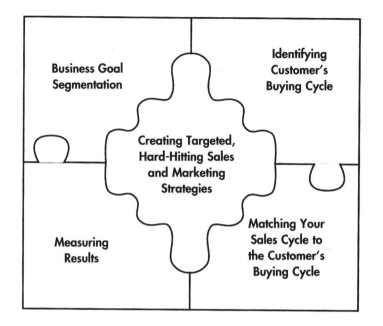

are assembling the puzzle, we might find that we are missing information and cannot complete the puzzle. It is then our responsibility to fill in the missing information so that we can produce the best sales and marketing strategy that we can. We will be going through the next several sections to create a targeted, hard-hitting sales and marketing strategy.

THE ROI-BASED SALES AND MARKETING PROCESS

Establish Your Goals

Chapter 4—Business Goal Segmentation
Before you can begin to determine your sales and marketing plan, you need to define success. What products are you selling? in what geographies? in what industries? through what channels of distribution? to whom? We can't claim a victory unless we know what it means. Business Goal Segmentation helps you to clearly segment your market so that you know what your ultimate target really is.

Profile Your Target Customer Audience

Chapter 5—Profiling the Ideal Prospect: Segmenting Your Market
Once you have defined what your objectives are, you now need to profile your ideal prospects. Who are they? Where are they? What's important to them? Who is most critical to your success?

Define What the Customer Must Do in Order to Buy

Chapter 6—Identifying Your Customer's Buying Cycle
What is this specific customer's Buying Cycle? What must the customer do in order to buy? How many customers do you need at each stage of the Buying Cycle? How long will it take a customer to move through this Buying Cycle?

Develop Your Marketing Strategy to Make It Happen

Chapter 7—Matching Your Sales Cycle to the Customer's Buying Cycle
Now let's look at your actions. What will you say? What will you do? and What will you measure to move your customer through his or her Buying Cycle as quickly and efficiently as possible?

Be Sure You Are Marketing to All of the Appropriate Audiences

Chapter 8—How to Deal with Multiple Audiences
There are many audiences that you need to market to besides the decision makers. How about influencers (such as the press and consultants) and recommenders (such as a technical recommender or a financial adviser)? When you market to multiple audiences, you need to be sure that you understand their role in the overall Buying Cycle and how you can market to them so that they can execute that role.

Execute the Strategy

Chapter 9—Creating Hard-Hitting and On-Target Sales and Marketing Strategies
As you begin to implement your strategy, make sure that it is optimal. Are the activities that you have chosen the best to move the customer

through the Buying Cycle as quickly and efficiently as possible? Do you need to change your messages or your actions or some of your internal processes to gain maximum efficiency and effectiveness?

Manage Your Plan

Chapter 10—Measuring the Results You Get

Here's our radical statement. Because companies are so activities-driven, they sometimes can't believe that we encourage them to do less in a more focused manner. Why? Because more activity does not necessarily mean more revenue or more results. And, if a company does a lot of Sales and Marketing activities but does not measure the results of those activities, what have they gained? More expense and no way of knowing if they were successful. Here's the bottom line: Targeted, focused Sales and Marketing activities that are aimed at the customer's Buying Cycle and are measured will give you more results and more revenue.

> **IF YOU'RE NOT GOING TO MEASURE YOUR SALES AND MARKETING ACTIVITIES, DON'T BOTHER DOING THEM BECAUSE YOU WON'T KNOW IF YOU'VE SUCCEEDED OR NOT. YOU'RE WASTING YOUR TIME.**

The point is that Marketing is very often a nebulous blob. It's like a marshmallow. You punch it, and it bounces right back. It's hard to make a dent. The only way you can prove you are successful is to measure your results. Measurement should take only 2–5% of your overall project time.

Report Your Sales and Marketing Results

Chapter 11—Reporting Your Results

Many people have been conditioned by their companies not to be held accountable for their results. So, the behavior that is encouraged is simply either to not report at all or, if they report, to tell only the good news. This is extremely dangerous for obvious reasons. How can the management of the company make changes and adjustments to a sales and marketing strategy if they do not know where they really stand? In this chapter, we have included a Marketing Reporting Template and a Sales Forecast Model. If used, these two vehicles will tell you exactly:

- where your customers are in their Buying Cycle
- how much money you have spent to date
- what activities you have done to date
- what sales messages you have used to move customers through the Buying Cycle to date
- what revenue you really can expect and when you will have it

Manage Your Time, Money and People

Chapter 12—Measuring/Managing Your Resources

Here's the final point. People will do only what you measure them and value them to do. If you reward an activities mentality, that's what you'll get: lots of activities. If you value a return-on-investment mentality, that is also what you'll get: commitment to focus on the customer, the customer's Buying Cycle and the measurement/movement of the customer through that Buying Cycle. The choice is up to you. To our way of thinking, though, it is much less stressful to drive an organization with an ROI mentality than with an activities mentality. It is also less costly.

The choice is yours.

An Example You Can Follow

Chapter 13—An Example of a Complete Plan

Part Two concludes with an example of a completed plan for Compu-Sys, a fictitious manufacturing company. CompuSys is based on the hundreds of companies we have worked with. The plan is an excellent template for you to follow when you create your company's business plan. By applying the concepts of CompuSys's plan to your business, you will create a business plan that focuses on driving your revenue with the *correct* Sales and Marketing activities. You can be sure that your plan gives you the best ROI possible on your Sales and Marketing investment. You will *know* that you can profitably sell and market a particular product or service *prior* to spending money on Sales or Marketing.

PART TWO

METHODOLOGY—
THE ROAD MAP
TO AVOID PITFALLS

In Part Two we will focus on the ROI-Based Sales and Marketing methodology. We will examine what you need to do in order to create an ROI-Based Sales and Marketing plan. Chapters 4–12 will provide you with the tools you need to create your own profit-driven business plan. The use of these tools will help to ensure your success.

A few years ago there was a humorous commercial in which a customer of a hamburger fast food company repeatedly asked, Where's the beef? Part Two truly is the beef of Sales and Marketing. If your company implements the concepts outlined here, you will be placing yourself ahead of your competition. You will maximize your productivity. You will generate more revenue and profit. In short, you will be a hero.

Before you begin Part Two, however, it is imperative that you determine the health of your own Sales and Marketing organizations. We have provided a Sales and Marketing Self-Health Test on page 234 in the Appendix, which we ask that you take now. This test will help you to determine the strengths and weaknesses of your Sales and Marketing organizations. By answering the questions in the self-health test, you will be able to get a feel for where fixes should be applied within your Sales and Marketing organizations. The content in Part Two will then give you a framework on how to implement these fixes within your company.

Establish Your Goals:
Business Goal Segmentation

4

*B*efore we begin to profile our ideal prospect and examine his or her Buying Cycle, we need to segment our revenue and our markets. The reason we do this is so that we are very clear what success is. How many customers do you need to sell a particular product to? in what industries? in what geographies?

If you set your objectives too broadly, it is very difficult to measure success and sometimes you won't even be able to tell if you came close to achieving it. We'll use the following analogy to demonstrate the point. Let's say that I want to go from New York to California. How can I get there? California is an awfully big place. I guess I could just point my car west and drive. Eventually I'll get there, but is anywhere in California OK? Does it matter if I end up in Los Angeles and I really would have preferred to be in San Francisco?

Too often, people in Marketing do not make specific enough goals. Or they make very broad goals (generate $xxx billion in revenue) but they have no idea how to get there from here.

QUESTION: How do you eat an elephant?
ANSWER: One bite at a time.
SUGGESTION: Break down your revenue objectives into bite-size pieces so that you know when you have achieved success.

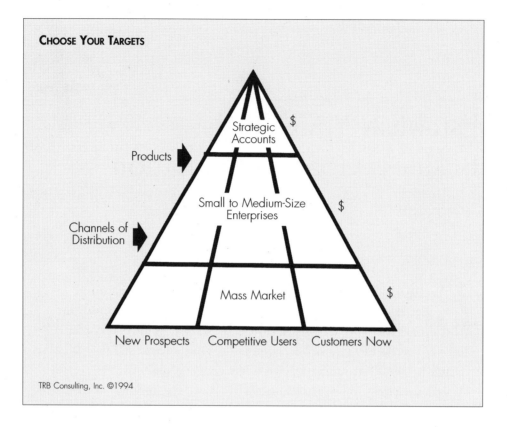

CHOOSE YOUR TARGETS

Strategic Accounts

Products

Small to Medium-Size Enterprises

Channels of Distribution

Mass Market

New Prospects   Competitive Users   Customers Now

TRB Consulting, Inc. ©1994

To go back to our California analogy, let's say that our ultimate objective is to get to San Francisco from New York. Let's also say we're going to go by car. Now, we can map out our path. We can say what cities we should get to by what time. We can definitely assess our progress, and we can declare success as we move toward our ultimate objective.

Look at the diagram "Choose Your Targets." Markets can be split between strategic accounts (for instance, the Fortune 500 or the Fortune 1000), small to medium-size companies, and the mass market. Your strategy may vary depending on the market you go after. You might sell certain products to certain markets. You might use several channels of distribution (ways of reaching the end consumer) for the various targeted markets.

We can guarantee that your sales messages would be different for new prospects versus your customers today (who know you and love you). We also know that they would probably be different for a prospect who is using your competitor's product.

The point is that Marketing is indeed often very broad. In order to be effective, you must analyze *where* your revenue will come from so you will know *how* to market most effectively.

Let's apply this further. Each of your products/services may have to be marketed differently. There may be different factors for each product set. For instance:

- What is your channel of distribution? Will you market this product internally or externally? with an internal sales force or with a reseller?
- Are there different classes of buyers? If there are, will each need to be marketed to differently? Will your sales messages be different?
- Are you selling this product into different industries? Do you need to market differently for each different industry?
- Are you marketing to a new prospect or to an installed customer? Would you market to each differently?

So, the first step in marketing successfully is to segment your business. We call this Business Goal Segmentation—the quantification of objectives in such a way that you can understand the number of customers who must buy to meet goals.

- What is your revenue goal?
- How does it break down by product, geography, channel of distribution, industry and class of customer?

One of our customers recently suggested that Business Goal Segmentation makes much more sense to that customer's organization when they think of it as revenue mix analysis. No matter what you call it, *the objective is to understand how many people you need to buy your product or service.* Where will the revenue come from?

- Which products?
- Which geographies?
- Which industries?
- Which types of customers (new customers, your installed base, competitive users)?

How Business Goal Segmentation Works

Business Goal Segmentation is one of the most important things that you can do to define what success is to your company or organization. It will help you to focus on your end objective—revenue—and it will help you determine how many sales you need to make in order to be successful. Here are the steps that you need to take in order to create your own Business Goal Segmentation.

Step	Action	Description
1	Determine your revenue objectives.	Include this fiscal year plus the next two years' revenue objectives.
2	Determine targeted geographies.	Include percentage of revenue expected and actual dollar amount of revenue expected.
3	List products and services.	List specific products and services along with percentage and dollar amount expected.
4	Determine which industry you will sell each of the products and services.	Include the average sales price and number of sales needed.

≈≈≈

> ### IF YOU DON'T DETERMINE WHAT YOUR BUSINESS GOALS ARE (WHAT SUCCESS IS), YOU'LL NEVER KNOW IF YOU'VE SUCCEEDED. IT'S VITAL TO DO A BUSINESS GOAL SEGMENTATION BEFORE PROCEEDING.

The following worksheets have been included to help you with your own Business Goal Segmentation.

Step 1—Determine Revenue Objectives

Current Fiscal Year	Fiscal Year +1	Fiscal Year +2

Step 2—Determine Targeted Geographies

Complete the above worksheet for each fiscal year you identified in step 1. (If you are selling into only one geography, then skip step 2 and go to step 3.)

Geography	% of Revenue Expected	$ Expected
Total	100%	$

Step 3—Identify the Products or Services That Will Achieve Your Revenue Objectives

Product or Service	Geography _____	Geography _____	Geography _____	Total Revenue
	$ _____ _____ %	$ _____ _____ %	$ _____ _____ %	$ _____ _____ %
	$ _____ _____ %	$ _____ _____ %	$ _____ _____ %	$ _____ _____ %
	$ _____ _____ %	$ _____ _____ %	$ _____ _____ %	$ _____ _____ %
TOTAL	$ _____ _____ %	$ _____ _____ %	$ _____ _____ %	$ _____ 100%

The number of rows and columns is totally dependent on your business. If you are selling into one geography with three products or services, then you would need to fill in the column for only one geography. If you have more than three products, use the table provided in the Appendix.

Be sure to complete this worksheet for each fiscal year you identified in step 1.

Step 4—Identify the Industries to Which You Will Sell Your Product/Service

This next worksheet should be used to help you prioritize where you should focus your efforts. You probably cannot focus on everything down to the finest detail. Therefore, this worksheet will help you to say, "I will focus here, here and here. The rest is not as important." The way you choose the most important things to you is to ask yourself the following questions.

- Which products/services are driving the bulk of our revenue?
- Are we entering a new market? If so, then do we have to invest more sales and marketing effort to bring the product to a steady run rate?
- Are we phasing our company to run from one channel of distribution to another?
- Which products, industries, geographies, channels of distribution are most important to us?

You probably can't do it all, so, prioritize your efforts.

The step 4 worksheet is also extremely versatile. Once you have completed step 3, you can use this worksheet to look at:

- The industries that you will sell into for a particular product
- The class of buyers that you will sell to for a particular product
- The channels of distribution that you will use for a particular product

Note: Complete one worksheet for each product or service that you have identified in step 3. Using the step 4 worksheet, be sure to determine how many sales you will need for a particular product itself, or industry within a product, or class of buyer within a product or channel of distribution within a product.

If an industry cut is important to your business, use the following worksheet.

Product _____	Geography _____	Geography _____	Total Revenue
Industry:	$ _____ _____ % Avg. Sale Price = $ _____ # of Sales Needed = _____	$ _____ _____ % Avg. Sale Price = $ _____ # of Sales Needed = _____	$ _____ _____ %
Industry:	$ _____ _____ % Avg. Sale Price = $ _____ # of Sales Needed = _____	$ _____ _____ % Avg. Sale Price = $ _____ # of Sales Needed = _____	$ _____ _____ %

If a class of buyer (i.e., consumers, small businesses, large corporations) cut is important to your business, use this worksheet.

Product _____	Geography _____	Geography _____	Total Revenue
Class of buyer:	$ _____ _____ % Avg. Sale Price = $ _____ # of Sales Needed = _____	$ _____ _____ % Avg. Sale Price = $ _____ # of Sales Needed = _____	$ _____ _____ %
Class of buyer:	$ _____ _____ % Avg. Sale Price = $ _____ # of Sales Needed = _____	$ _____ _____ % Avg. Sale Price = $ _____ # of Sales Needed = _____	$ _____ _____ %

If a channel of distribution (i.e., internal sales force, resellers) cut is important to your business, use this worksheet.

Product _____	Geography _____	Geography _____	Total Revenue
Channel of distribution:	$ _____ _____ % Avg. Sale Price = $ _____ # of Sales Needed = _____	$ _____ _____ % Avg. Sale Price = $ _____ # of Sales Needed = _____	$ _____ _____ %
Channel of distribution:	$ _____ _____ % Avg. Sale Price = $ _____ # of Sales Needed = _____	$ _____ _____ % Avg. Sale Price = $ _____ # of Sales Needed = _____	$ _____ _____ %

To see precisely how these worksheets can be used, we have provided a case study of XYZ Company, which we will refer to throughout this book.

TAILORING THE WORKSHEETS TO MEET YOUR BUSINESS NEEDS

Although we have provided suggestions on how to cut your Business Goal Segmentation, be aware that you may choose to look at your company differently than we have suggested. For example,

- perhaps you sell into only one geography—the United States, and
- perhaps you need to cut your data by products within a channel of distribution

If so, just modify steps 2 and 3 as follows.

Step 1—Determine Revenue Objectives

Current Fiscal Year	Fiscal Year +1	Fiscal Year +2

Step 2—Determine Targeted Channel of Distribution

Channel of Distribution	% of Revenue Expected	$ Expected
Total	100%	$

Step 3—Identify the Products or Services That Will Achieve Your Revenue Objectives

Product or Service	Geography _____	Geography _____	Geography _____	Total Revenue
	$ _____ _____ %	$ _____ _____ %	$ _____ _____ %	$ _____ _____ %
	$ _____ _____ %	$ _____ _____ %	$ _____ _____ %	$ _____ _____ %
	$ _____ _____ %	$ _____ _____ %	$ _____ _____ %	$ _____ _____ %
Total	$ _____ _____ %	$ _____ _____ %	$ _____ _____ %	$ _____ 100%

You can change any of the variables on any of the worksheets. It depends on what is important to you in your business.

XYZ COMPANY EXAMPLE—BUSINESS GOAL SEGMENTATION

XYZ Company is an international company that manufactures quite a few discrete products:

- widgets
- gizmos
- whirligigs
- propellers

The current fiscal year's revenue is projected at $5 million. Next year, XYZ expects to grow 10%. The following is an example of XYZ's current-year Business Goal Segmentation.

Step 1—Determine Revenue Objectives

Current Fiscal Year	Fiscal Year +1	Fiscal Year +2
$5,000,000	$5,500,000	$6,500,000

Step 2—Determine Targeted Geographies

CURRENT YEAR:

Geography	% of Revenue Expected	$ Expected
United States	50%	$2.50M
France	10%	$0.50M
Italy	15%	$0.75M
Japan	25%	$1.25M
Total	100%	$5.00M

Step 3—Identify the Products or Services That Will Achieve Your Revenue Objectives

Product or Service	United States	France	Italy	Japan	Total Revenue
Widgets	$1.25M 50%	$100K 20%	$187.5K 25%	$937.5K 75%	$2,475,000 49.5%
Gizmos	$625K 25%	$375K 75%	$375K 50%	$312.5K 25%	$1,687,500 33.75%
Whirligigs	$250K 10%	$25K 5%	$75K 10%	$0 0%	$350,000 7%
Propellers	$375K 15%	$0 0%	$112.5K 15%	$0 0%	$487,500 9.75%
Total	$2.5M 100%	$.5M 100%	$.75M 100%	$1.25M 100%	$5.0M 100%

Step 4—Identify the Industries to Which You Will Sell Your Product/Service

CURRENT YEAR:

As you can see from step 3, widgets are clearly the most important product in XYZ's portfolio. They will account for 49.5% of this year's revenue. So, let's focus on widgets in this example. XYZ will be selling widgets mostly into the chemical and pharmaceutical industries. Here is what this year's Business Goal Segmentation looks like for widgets.

Product: Widgets	United States	France	Italy	Japan	Total Revenue
Industry: Chemicals	$937.5K 75% Avg. Sale Price = $2500 # of Sales Needed = 375	$50K 50% Avg. Sale Price = $2500 # of Sales Needed = 20	$56.25K 30% Avg. Sale Price = $2500 # of Sales Needed = 23	$468.75K 50% Avg. Sale Price = $2500 # of Sales Needed = 188	$1,512.5K 61.1%
Industry: Pharma-ceuticals	$250K 20% Avg. Sale Price = $2500 # of Sales Needed = 100	$50K 50% Avg. Sale Price = $2500 # of Sales Needed = 20	$131.25K 70% Avg. Sale Price = $2500 # of Sales Needed = 52.5	$375K 40% Avg. Sale Price = $2500 # of Sales Needed = 150	$806.25K 32.6%
Industry: Other	$62.5K 5% Avg. Sale Price = $2500 # of Sales Needed = 25	$0 0% Avg. Sale Price = N/A # of Sales Needed = N/A	$0 0% Avg. Sale Price = N/A # of Sales Needed = N/A	$93.75K 10% Avg. Sale Price = 2500 # of Sales Needed = 38	$156.25K 6.3%

XYZ is going to sell its widgets through two channels of distribution:

- Its direct sales force
- A reseller who is familiar with its markets

Product: Widgets	United States	France	Italy	Japan	Total Revenue
Channel of distribution: Internal Sales Force	$1,000K 80% Avg. Sale Price = $2500 # of Sales Needed = 400	$20K 20% Avg. Sale Price = $2500 # of Sales Needed = 8	$56.25K 30% Avg. Sale Price = $2500 # of Sales Needed = 23	$562.5K 60% Avg. Sale Price = $2500 # of Sales Needed = 225	$1,638.75K 66.2%
Channel of distribution: Reseller	$250K 20% Avg. Sale Price = $2500 # of Sales Needed = 100	$80K 80% Avg. Sale Price = $2500 # of Sales Needed = 32	$131.25K 70% Avg. Sale Price = $2500 # of Sales Needed = 52.5	$375K 40% Avg. Sale Price = $2500 # of Sales Needed = 150	$836.25K 33.8%

XYZ has ascertained that there are really three classes of buyers who buy their products:

- Large corporations
- Small to medium-size companies
- Home consumers

Here is the Business Goal Segmentation for class of buyer within product (widgets):

Product: Widgets	United States	France	Italy	Japan	Total Revenue
Class of buyer: Large Corporations	$625K 50% Avg. Sale Price = $10,000 # of Sales Needed = 62.5	$20K 20% Avg. Sale Price = $7500 # of Sales Needed = 3	$56.25K 30% Avg. Sale Price = $7500 # of Sales Needed = 8	$468.75K 50% Avg. Sale Price = $12,000 # of Sales Needed = 39	$1,170K 47.3%
Class of buyer: Small to Medium-Size Companies	$500K 40% Avg. Sale Price = $2500 # of Sales Needed = 200	$50K 50% Avg. Sale Price = $2000 # of Sales Needed = 25	$112.5K 60% Avg. Sale Price = $2000 # of Sales Needed = 57	$375K 40% Avg. Sale Price = $2500 # of Sales Needed = 150	$1,037.5K 41.9%
Class of buyer: Home Consumers	$125K 10% Avg. Sale Price = $1000 # of Sales Needed = 125	$30K 30% Avg. Sale Price = $750 # of Sales Needed = 40	$18.75K 10% Avg. Sale Price = $500 # of Sales Needed = 38	$93.75K 10% Avg. Sale Price = $1500 # of Sales Needed = 63	$267.5K 10.8%

Based on the foregoing information, XYZ has come to the following decisions.

- It will focus its direct sales force to sell into the large and medium-size corporations.
- It will direct its resellers to sell into the small corporations and home consumer marketplace.

- It will put together marketing campaigns and efforts directed to the chemical and pharmaceutical industries—particularly in the United States and Japan.
- It must put more effort into the resellers market in Italy and France. In fact, upon doing this analysis, XYZ ascertained that currently, it does not have the proper resellers signed up in Japan, Italy or France to sell to the numbers of customers needed to succeed.

PROJECTING BUSINESS TRENDS

Business Goal Segmentation is especially useful when used to compare two fiscal years (the current year and next year). By looking at how many sales are needed by product within a geography from one year to the next, you can tell if you have adequate resources to meet the demand. You can also determine if your growth projections are reasonable and doable.

KEY LEARNINGS CHECKLIST

☑ Make sure you've identified your business goals—particularly your revenue targets for the next two to three years. You won't know whether you've been successful if you haven't established a target.

☑ Setting a broad, large revenue goal is not enough. Further break the revenue down by either:

- Product
- Geography
- Industry
- Channel of distribution (internal sales versus resellers versus direct marketing methods)
- Class of buyer (new customer, your installed base, competitive users)

The way you slice and dice your revenue is purely up to you. What makes the most business sense?

☑ The bottom line is: How many customers *must* buy in order for you to be successful?

If you don't know the answer to this, you won't know if you're on target or off. You may be generating revenue, but you may not know how you got there. This is dangerous.

Profiling the Ideal Prospect: Segmenting Your Market

5

Now that you have completed your Business Goal Segmentation, you have defined what success is. You know how many customers you need to sell to for a particular product, industry, channel of distribution or class of buyer.

The next important thing to do is to clearly define who your ideal prospect is for each product or service that you have identified in your Business Goal Segmentation.

This is important. You might have different customers for different products. Therefore it is vital to know to whom you are selling (what they need, who they are, what job they are doing, what keeps them awake at night) in order to be successful.

Who is this person that you are trying to sell to? Customers are people. Thank goodness! We can talk to people. We can figure out who they are, where they are, what's important to them, what is compelling them to need our product or service.

Notice that in the chart on the following page, "Profile Your Target Customer Audience," we recommend that you identify your ideal prospect's title. There are several reasons for doing this.

First of all, a Vice President of Engineering at one pharmaceutical company probably has the same issues/concerns as the Vice President of Engineering in a competitive firm. So, if we know the title, we can iden-

---

PROFILE YOUR
TARGET CUSTOMER AUDIENCE

- By Title
- By Geography
- By Industry
- By Company Size
- By Customer Type (Installed base, New account, Competitive user)
- By Common Issues/Concerns

TRB Consulting Group, Inc. ©1994

---

tify common sales messages addressed to what keeps your customers awake at night.

Second, by knowing the titles of our customers, list acquisition becomes so much easier.

Third, it helps you to think of your prospects as *people* instead of markets. *People* make decisions, not companies or markets.

So, too, as we market understanding the title of our ideal prospects, we must also know their geography, their industry, their company size and their customer type (from our installed base, a new customer, a competitive user). This helps us to target our customers for list purposes, but it also helps us to identify the actions that the customer must take in order to buy. Once we know who the customers are and what actions they must take, that helps us to further target the sales messages we will use to move these customers through the Buying Cycle as quickly and efficiently as possible.

≋ 1. WHOM DO YOU WANT TO TAKE ACTION? ≋

Answer the following questions in the next section.

DESCRIBE YOUR PROSPECTS

- Identify *whom* you will be selling to, *by title*:

TITLE

Decision maker   _____

Financial approver   _____

Technical evaluator   _____

Recommender   _____

Approver   _____

Champion   _____

We use the following definitions:

Decision Maker
- Someone who will find the business aspects of your product or service most important
- Someone who will find the technical aspects of your product or service most important

Influencer
- Might be some internal job title within the customer's company that can influence the decision maker, or it might be . . .
  — Press
  — Analysts

Recommender
- Some internal job titles within the customer's company whose recommendation is vital to close the sale. Might be a technical evaluation team.

Approver
- Many times this is a financial person who is not involved in the decision but could very easily veto the purchase if he or she has not adequately been marketed to

Champion
- The person in the company who would most benefit from your product and would be likely to champion it inside the company to key decision makers or influencers

Describe the factors that will help you qualify prospects (revenue, number of employees, profits, number of locations, budget, etc.):

_____

_____

Describe where the prospects are located (territory, city, state/province, country, worldwide):

_____

_____

Describe which industries or segments are the best prospects, or describe other factors that might influence your strategy (industries, your installed base, a competitive installed base, etc.):

_____

_____

_____

Based on the above, who is *most* critical to your success? (usually the ultimate decision maker, who should be the focal point of your selling efforts):
Title: _____

List the secondary target(s) of your sales and marketing strategy:
Title: _____
Title: _____

The answering of the foregoing questions can also help you a great deal if you need to acquire a list to market to. You now know:

- Whom you want to market to: the titles of individuals
- What geographies, industries, size of company and other factors are important

It can also be helpful to define who is not an ideal prospect. What titles of people would be most adverse to or threatened by your product or service? Are there certain traits that people have that would make them less desirous of your product or service?

Here's an example. One of our clients was selling a new and revolutionary product that could really impact its customers' bottom line. Our customer's current strategy was to sell this product to low- to mid-level managers. After working through *The Buck Starts Here*, the client decided that the customers it should be calling on had to be much more senior level managers—people who were innovators or early adopters. It could not target late adopters or laggards—people who were risk averse. Because the product could give customers significant competitive advantages, our client needed to target aggressive, young companies that had aggressive, young management teams.

If you are trying to sell something that is new and revolutionary to someone who is a late adopter or a laggard, your chances of success may be greatly reduced. You may need to target an innovator or an early adopter.

Be sure you know who is a good prospect and who is a bad one.

XYZ Company Example—Profiling XYZ's Ideal Prospect

Let's go back to XYZ Company.

Remember in the Business Goal Segmentation example in Chapter 4 that XYZ determined that widgets were its best-selling product? Widgets accounted for 49.5% of overall sales worldwide. In fact, widgets in the United States would drive 25% of XYZ's total current fiscal-year goal.

Obviously, widgets are extremely important to XYZ's success. So let's look at the U.S. widget plan.

DEVELOPING SUCCESSFUL SALES AND MARKETING STRATEGIES: XYZ COMPANY

Describe Your Business Objectives

- Sales and Marketing strategy for:
  Widgets. We plan to drive $1.25M in widgets in the United States this fiscal year. We will focus this plan on selling $625K to large corporations in the United States.

- Product:
  The average sale price of a widget is $2,500. However, larger corporations tend to buy more, with an average sale price of $10,000 each. Small to medium-size companies buy with an average sales price of $2,500 each. Home consumers buy at an average sales price of $1,000 each.

  We will focus this plan on selling our widgets to 63 large corporations in the United States (at an average sales price of $10,000 each).

  Total Revenue for this Plan: $625,000
  For the Period Beginning 1/96, Ending 12/96

≋ 1. WHOM DO YOU WANT TO TAKE ACTION? ≋

Describe Your Prospects

- Identify whom you will be selling to, by title:

	TITLE
Decision maker	VP, Engineering
Financial approver	CFO
Influencer	VP, Manufacturing
Technical evaluator	Engineering manager
Recommender	Same as Technical evaluator
Approver	Same as Decision maker

- **Describe the factors that will help you qualify prospects** (revenue, number of employees, profits, number of locations, budget, etc.): *Companies with greater than $100M in sales and with greater than 50 manufacturing plants.*

- **Describe where the prospects are located** (territory, city, state/province, country, worldwide): *United States, though most are located in major metropolitan areas such as New York, Chicago, Detroit, and Los Angeles.*

- **Describe which industries or segments are the best prospects, or describe other factors that might influence your strategy** (industries, your installed base, a competitive installed base, etc.): *Due to the thrust of this product, we will focus on selling to new accounts. Since our product is new and state-of-the-art, there are no major competitors that we wish to displace.*

Based on the above, who is *most* critical to your success? (Usually the ultimate decision maker, who should be the focal point of your selling efforts):
   Title: VP, Engineering

List the secondary target(s) of your Sales and Marketing strategy:
   Title: VP, Manufacturing
   Title: CFO

KEY LEARNINGS CHECKLIST

☑ It is important to know *to whom* you are selling and marketing.

☑ By identifying the customer's title, location, company size, industry and type of buyer, we are better able to:

- Acquire a list of names to market to.
- Have our sales messages target what keeps the customer awake at night.

6

Identifying Your Customer's Buying Cycle

As we have said all along, current Sales and Marketing practices are usually extremely egocentric. We tend to focus exclusively on *our* actions—usually just on what *we* will do. By focusing on the customer and the customer's Buying Cycle, we will increase the efficiency of our Sales Cycle. Our targeted sales messages and activities will propel the customers to move forward in their Buying Cycles faster and in greater numbers.

The premises of *The Buck Starts Here* are to focus on the customer first—and on our actions (what we will say, do and measure) second.

So far we've:

- Defined what success is through Business Goal Segmentation.
- Targeted our ideal prospects (who they are, where they are, what is important to them).

Now we will focus on the customer's Buying Cycle. We define the customer's Buying Cycle as follows:

The customer's buying cycle consists of those actions that the customer must *take in order to buy.*

Customers quite often go through various stages of a Buying Cycle prior to actually purchasing a product or having an ongoing relationship with their vendor (such as "be a reference" or "be a testimonial").

The stages of a Buying Cycle that a customer typically goes through are as follows.

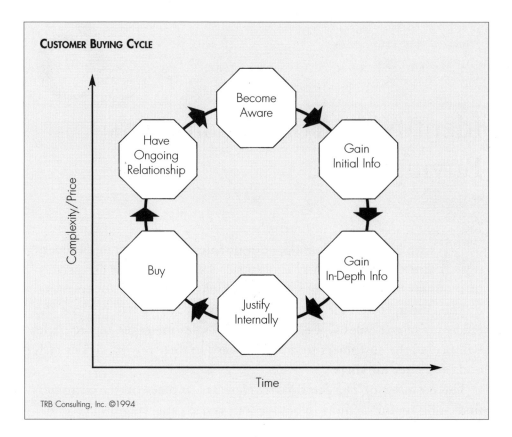

Customers usually start at Become Aware and move through the Buying Cycle until they purchase or use the product on an ongoing basis. Many times, once customers have used a product or service, they are predisposed to become aware of additional products or services that you might have. Your best prospects are your installed customers.

Many times, as the complexity or price of the product or service increases, so does the time it takes a customer to buy.

EXAMINE YOUR OWN BUYING CYCLE

Let's examine your own Buying Cycle. Let's imagine that you are buying an expensive product. Let's say it's a house. Here are what your actions will typically be.

STAGE OF BUYING CYCLE	YOUR ACTIONS
Become Aware	You check out various neighborhoods. You start to become aware of what you like and what you don't like about certain areas.
Gain Initial Information	You start looking at quite a few houses. You start narrowing down to a few that you want more information on.
Gain In-Depth Information	You really start gaining in-depth information on a handful of houses. Perhaps you consider: • The schools • The houses of worship • The neighbors/the neighborhood • The commute to work • The actual house itself: How is it structurally? Does it have termites?
Justify Internally	You go to the bank and see if you can get a mortgage. Can you afford this house?
Buy	You buy the house.
Ongoing Relationship	You live there a while. You love it and you tell friends and family about your neighborhood. Your in-laws move in next door. (Just kidding).

So, the more complex and expensive the product or service, typically the longer the customer's Buying Cycle.

Customers will usually go through each stage of a Buying Cycle. However, when we market to customers, we may be able to move them through the multiple stages of their Buying Cycle with very few marketing activities. For instance, if we are selling a very inexpensive, simple product, the customer may be able to gain initial information, gain in-depth information and even justify internally through a catalog. Therefore, the marketing activities we choose are extremely important in streamlining how effectively and efficiently a customer moves through the Buying Cycle. However, it is also extremely important not to choose the marketing activity before examining the customer's Buying Cycle. You might choose a marketing activity that seems obvious but upon examination does not have as good a return on investment as another marketing activity. There are many factors to consider before choosing the appropriate marketing activity. (We will get into much more detail on the selection of our marketing activities in the next chapter.)

THE STAGES OF A CUSTOMER'S BUYING CYCLE

Let's compare the stages of a customer's Buying Cycle to moving the customers through a pipeline.

The Business of Sales and Marketing

Buyers

Moving through the Pipeline

Implement

Buy

Financial Justification

In-Depth Analysis

Basic Fact Finding

Awareness

Prospects

If You Don't Know the Buying Cycle . . .

TRB Consulting Group, Inc. ©1994

The customer moves from awareness to basic fact finding to in-depth analysis to financial justification to buying the product or service to implementing/using the product or service. Once we identify the customer's Buying Cycle, then we will establish a Sales Cycle that matches to the customer's Buying Cycle. Our purpose is to move the customer through his or her Buying Cycle as quickly and efficiently as possible.

The Business of Sales and Marketing

Buyers

The Sales Cycle

Sell More	
Install	Implement
Close	Buy
Convince	Financial Justification
Qualify	In-Depth Analysis
Prospect	Basic Fact Finding
Suspect	Awareness

Prospects

. . . How Can You Make It Happen?

TRB Consulting Group, Inc. ©1994

If we examine what Sales and Marketing organizations ideally should do together, they should:

- Market to suspects to make them aware so that Sales and Marketing can move the customers up the Buying Cycle to do basic fact finding.

- Market to prospects to give them basic fact-finding information so that the customer can move up the Buying Cycle to in-depth analysis.
- And so on

Once we know the customer's Buying Cycle, then we will focus on our Sales Cycle. As we said previously, many companies begin with the Sales Cycle (what you will *do* to get the customer to buy). This is very egocentric and can be misleading. If you focus on you first, how will you know who the customer is, what the customer needs and how the customer wants to be marketed to?

At *each* state of the customer's Buying Cycle (Awareness, Basic Fact Finding, etc.) we will determine *how we will sell* to the customer. We will develop our Sales Cycle to match the customer's Buying Cycle.

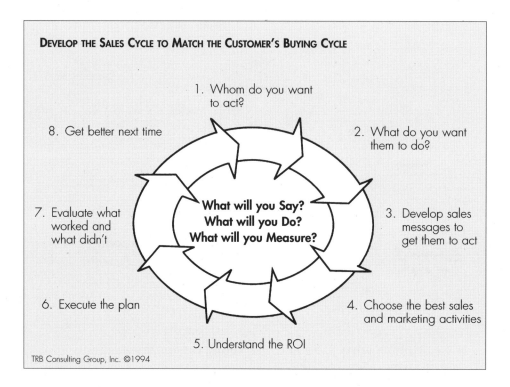

DEVELOP THE SALES CYCLE TO MATCH THE CUSTOMER'S BUYING CYCLE

1. Whom do you want to act?
2. What do you want them to do?
3. Develop sales messages to get them to act
4. Choose the best sales and marketing activities
5. Understand the ROI
6. Execute the plan
7. Evaluate what worked and what didn't
8. Get better next time

What will you Say? What will you Do? What will you Measure?

TRB Consulting Group, Inc. ©1994

(The Sales Cycle and the focus on our actions—what we will say, do and measure—will be explained in great detail in the next chapter.)

WHAT DOES THE CUSTOMER HAVE TO DO IN ORDER TO BUY?

- Ask for more information.
- Place an order.
- Get questions answered.
- Assign an evaluation team.
- Conduct a pilot.
- Request a proposal.
- Become aware.
- See a need.
- Acquire a belief.

TRB Consulting Group, Inc. ©1994

Let's continue with the analysis of our customer's Buying Cycle. Once we profile our customers (who they are, what is important to them), we then need to look at what actions the customer must take in order to buy or implement our product or service *and* we must figure out what stages of the customer's Buying Cycle these actions fit into. Each Buying Cycle created must be tailored to fit the customers it is addressing.

For different customer sets, these actions may be taken in different stages of the Buying Cycle. Where these actions fit in your marketplace depends on your customer set. The best way to know where they fit is to ask your sales force. They move customers through the Buying Cycle every day.

Why is it important to understand the actions that a customer must take in order to buy from you?

Well, first, you will identify the actions (then the stages of the Buying Cycle) that must take place. This will help you to target your sales and marketing activities—focused toward those customer actions.

Second, it helps you to identify any holes you might have in your resources. Maybe you don't have enough people or equipment in place to help customers take the action they need to take. This helps you to take corrective action.

Third, and most important, if you don't *know* what actions your customers must take, how can you help them?

≈≈ 2. WHAT DO YOU WANT THEM TO DO? ≈≈

Use the following worksheets to determine what actions your customer must take in order to buy.

WHAT DO YOU ULTIMATELY WANT THE CUSTOMER TO DO?

Describe your short-term and long-term goals for these prospects:

Short-term goals (e.g., buy a pilot, evaluate the product, buy an evaluation, buy the product):

_____

_____

_____

Long-term goals (e.g., become a good reference account, repeat buy, etc.):

_____

_____

_____

Describe the major checkpoints or buying actions the typical prospect will take to move through the Buying Cycle:

Actions

_____

_____

_____

_____

_____

Now, transfer those actions to the appropriate stage of the Customer Buying Cycle Worksheet shown below. Don't work yet on quantities of people needed at each stage of the Buying Cycle; also don't work on the time needed for a customer to move through the Buying Cycle. We'll do that next. Just fill in *where* the actions that your customer takes fit: at what stage of the Buying Cycle.

Note: Keep in mind that the Buying Cycle the decision maker goes through will be different from that of the technical evaluator or financial approver. Multiple Buying/Sales Cycles may be involved.

(We will discuss multiple Buying/Sales Cycles in Chapter 8, "How to Deal with Multiple Audiences.")

Customer Buying Cycle Worksheet

For_____

Total Revenue _____

Period Beginning _____

Period Ending _____

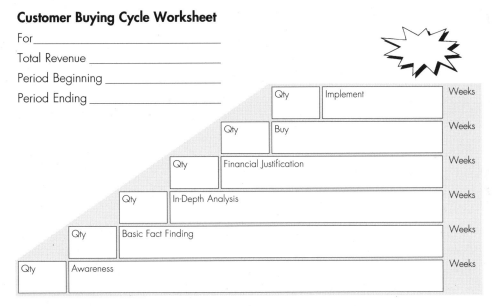

Qty	Implement	Weeks
Qty	Buy	Weeks
Qty	Financial Justification	Weeks
Qty	In-Depth Analysis	Weeks
Qty	Basic Fact Finding	Weeks
Qty	Awareness	Weeks

TRB Consulting Group, Inc. ©1994

Let's look at XYZ's filled-in Customer Buying Cycle Worksheet. The details of XYZ's customer's actions are found at the end of this chapter.

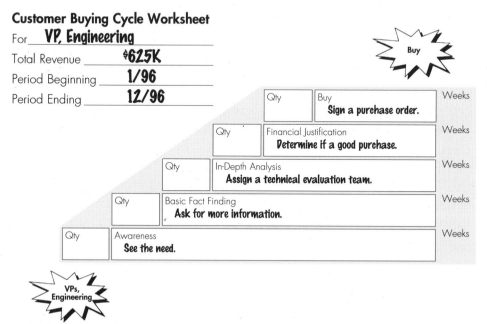

Customer Buying Cycle Worksheet
For **VP, Engineering**
Total Revenue   **$625K**
Period Beginning **1/96**
Period Ending   **12/96**

Buy

Qty	Buy — **Sign a purchase order.**	Weeks
Qty	Financial Justification — **Determine if a good purchase.**	Weeks
Qty	In-Depth Analysis — **Assign a technical evaluation team.**	Weeks
Qty	Basic Fact Finding — **Ask for more information.**	Weeks
Qty	Awareness — **See the need.**	Weeks

VPs, Engineering

TRB Consulting Group, Inc. ©1994

UNDERSTANDING THE METRICS

Once that you have determined the stages that your customer will go through in his or her Buying Cycle, you now need to determine:

- How many customers you need at each stage of the Buying Cycle.
- How long it will take for a customer to move through the Buying Cycle.
- Whether that meets your objectives.

Why is this important?

- By understanding how many customers are needed at each stage of the customer's Buying Cycle, we can count to see if we're on or off target. This means better forecasting and being assured that you'll hit your revenue objectives. In short, it ensures your peace of mind.

• By understanding how long it takes a typical customer to move through his or her Buying Cycle, we can determine whether that meets *our* objectives. If not, we can take corrective action. We must then ask ourselves, "What can we do or say to move the customer through his or her Buying Cycle faster?"

Quantifying How Many Customers Are Needed at Each Stage of a Buying Cycle

Now that your Buying Cycle has been designed, you need to determine how many customers/prospects you need in the target audience to take action at each stage of the Buying Cycle.

Steps to quantify the audience:

STEP	ACTION
1	Start with your short-term or long-term goal (from your Ideal Prospect Worksheet). How many people do you need to take this action?
2	Work *backward* from stage to stage down the Buying Cycle, estimating how many people you need at each stage. It is important to work backward, start at how many you need, and work your way backward.
3	Finish with how many people (customers) you need to start with.
4	Are there that many? Are the numbers realistic?

IF	THEN
Yes, the numbers are achievable.	Go to next step.
No, the numbers are not achievable.	Go back to step 1 and calculate more-accurate numbers, or determine if your plan is feasible.

> One of our customers commented:
> "The way I like to look at a situation is to look at what makes the cash register ring and work my way backward. That's what this approach does. It makes common sense."
>
> — Bob Welch
> Vice President of Sales

Many times people make the mistake of first starting with how many people they know exist in a certain marketplace and then they work their way up the Buying Cycle. This approach can be deceptive, because people can just fool themselves. They force-fit the numbers. Actually, the ideal situation is an iterative process whereby you work your way backward and then work your way forward to double-check your assumptions.

Many times people say, "We just don't know how many people to project at each stage. What should we do?" Our response is, "Put all of the right people in the room. Use your best collective judgment. You know your product and market better than anyone else. Make an educated guess for now. If you have no idea, then you need to do market research and collect customer data."

Time Line for a Customer's Buying Cycle—How Long Will It Take?

Estimate the time it will take for just one average customer in the target audience to move forward through each stage of the Buying Cycle.

In addition to calculating how long it will take for the customer to complete each stage, be sure to also consider each action that may fall under that stage of the Buying Cycle. For instance, during the basic fact-finding stage of the Buying Cycle, your customer might:

- Ask for more information.
- Look at various alternatives.
- Ask to speak to a sales rep.

You must consider how much time this entire stage of the Buying Cycle will take—in this instance, Basic Fact Finding.

Steps to Calculate the Time Line

Follow these steps to calculate how long it will take one average customer in the target audience to complete each stage of his or her Buying Cycle.

STEP	ACTION	DESCRIPTION
1	Start with the first stage—Awareness. How long will it take for one person to complete this stage and move to the next?	Use your best estimate of time; ranges are permitted.
2	Calculate the time needed for each stage of the Buying Cycle.	Look at the time needed for a customer to move through each stage.
3	Calculate the total time needed for the customer to move through the Buying Cycle	Look at the total time. Does this meet your objectives? If not, go back to make sure your estimates are correct.

Understanding the Metrics

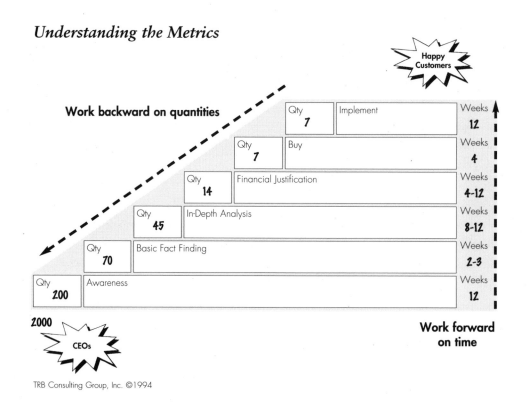

TRB Consulting Group, Inc. ©1994

This is what a completed customer Buying Cycle will look like. XYZ's completed customer Buying Cycle is at the end of this chapter.

WHAT TO DO IF YOU MIGHT NOT MEET YOUR DESIRED OBJECTIVES

As you work your way backward through the stages of the Buying Cycle from your short-term or long-term goal to how many people you need to start with, ask yourself the following questions.

- Are my estimates accurate?
- Have I involved on my team people who would know the answers?

If you find that you do not have enough people in your target audience to begin with, ask the following questions.

- Were we realistic in our estimates?
- If yes, should we consider expanding our audience to new industries? to new geographies? to new classes of buyers?

We had a client that was selling computer software to very large manufacturing companies. As the firm worked its way backward, it realized there were not enough customers to sell to. When we asked, "Are your numbers correct?" we were told, "Yes, all the right people are in this room. These estimates are accurate." The company decided to expand to other industries. It had previously been selling to the pharmaceutical and chemical industries. As a direct result of our session, the company decided to expand its focus to include the metals and glass industries.

If the customer does not move through the Buying Cycle quickly enough and you miss your objective, consider the following.

- Is there anything you could say or do that would move the customer through the Buying Cycle faster? (We will focus on this much more in the next chapter, "Matching Your Sales Cycle to the Customer's Buying Cycle.")
- Could you change your strategy so that the customer can take a few smaller actions that could add up to one very large action?

Here is an example of the latter point. We had a client that was trying to sell a very large systems integration project. The project was very expensive and the customer's Buying Cycle was extremely long. The Marketing and Sales team's objective was to bring in the business that fiscal year. However, the customer's Buying Cycle was to purchase in 18–24 months. Obviously, there was a mismatch. Once the team created an ROI-based sales and marketing plan, they realized they would need to change their strategy. The team decided to sell pieces of the integration project along the way. So instead of one very large sale, they phased the sale so that the customer could commit to smaller pieces faster.

XYZ Company Example: Identifying The Customer's Buying Cycle

≋ 2. What do you want them to do? ≋

Describe your short-term and long-term goals for these prospects:

Short-term Goals:
Buy a beginning purchase of our widgets ($10,000).

Long-term Goals:
- *Purchase more widgets next year so that a customer who has bought $10,000 this year will buy $20,000 next year.*
- *Be a reference.*

Describe the major checkpoints or buying actions the typical prospect will take to move through the Buying Cycle:

Actions

See the need for widgets.

Ask for more information.

Assign a team to evaluate our widgets.

Determine if our widgets are a good financial purchase.

Sign a purchase order.

Now, we've transferred these actions to the appropriate stage of the Customer Buying Cycle Worksheet (see next page).

Note: Keep in mind that the Buying Cycle the VP of Engineering goes through may be different from the VP of Manufacturing or the CFO. Multiple Buying/Sales Cycles will be involved in this example. (See Chapter 8, "How to Deal with Multiple Audiences.")

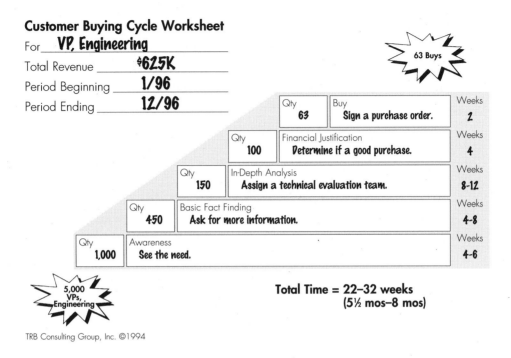

Customer Buying Cycle Worksheet

For **VP, Engineering**

Total Revenue **$625K**

Period Beginning **1/96**

Period Ending **12/96**

63 Buys

| Qty | Buy | Weeks |
| 63 | Sign a purchase order. | 2 |

| Qty | Financial Justification | Weeks |
| 100 | Determine if a good purchase. | 4 |

| Qty | In-Depth Analysis | Weeks |
| 150 | Assign a technical evaluation team. | 8-12 |

| Qty | Basic Fact Finding | Weeks |
| 450 | Ask for more information. | 4-8 |

| Qty | Awareness | Weeks |
| 1,000 | See the need. | 4-6 |

5,000 VPs, Engineering

Total Time = 22–32 weeks
(5½ mos–8 mos)

TRB Consulting Group, Inc. ©1994

KEY LEARNINGS CHECKLIST

☑ By identifying the customer's actions and their fit into the Buying Cycle, we will identify what the customer must do in order to buy. This helps us to direct our sales and marketing activities toward moving the customer through his or her Buying Cycle as quickly and efficiently as possible.

☑ By quantifying the number of Customers needed at each stage and working backward, we can determine:

1. If we're on or off target.
2. If there is a target customer population big enough for us to market to. If there isn't, we may need to expand our sales and marketing efforts to new industries, geographies or other types of customers.

☑ By determining the time frame that it will take a typical customer to move through the Buying Cycle, we can determine if we will meet *our* objectives (i.e., will enough customers buy by the end of our fiscal year?). If we realize that the Customer's Buying Cycle is very long, we might:

1. See if we can say or do anything to move the customer through the Buying Cycle faster.
2. Change our strategy so that the customer could take more small actions sooner (instead of one large action) that would add up to the total revenue needed but would bring in money faster.

Matching Your Sales Cycle to the Customer's Buying Cycle

*I*t is vital to think of your Sales Cycle as being an integral part of the customer's Buying Cycle. It does not stand alone. It does not come first. In fact, in order to be the most successful you can be, your Sales Cycle should be developed to perfectly match the customer's Buying Cycle. Your Sales Cycle should propel and compel the customer to move through his or her Buying Cycle as quickly and efficiently as possible. It should focus on what you will say, what you will do and what you will measure—the things that impact a customer and drive him or her to take action. Your choice of the best sales messages and activities that will deliver the best return on investment is what this chapter is all about.

So far we've:

1. Determined how you will segment your business by looking at what products or services will generate your revenue for the next fiscal year. We've also analyzed how many sales you need to make in each market segmentation in order for you to be successful.
2. Profiled your ideal prospect for your most important product.
3. Determined your customer's Buying Cycle (and quantified the number of customers needed at each stage of the Buying Cycle, determining the time it will take a customer to move through the Buying Cycle).

Please be aware that it is mandatory to do all of the previous steps *before* you determine your sales messages and sales and marketing activities. If you jump the gun and focus on your actions first, you might:

1. Give the *wrong sales message.*
2. Choose the *wrong sales and marketing activity.*
3. *Spend money on unneeded activities.*
4. *Not know if you're successful,* because you won't know what to count.

We are now ready to look at *your actions* (what you will say, what you will do and what you will measure).

Have you noticed that we haven't discussed any arty stuff so far? We've been discussing business and a business approach to Sales and Marketing. Actually, Marketing is both an art and a science. We don't want to take the art out of Marketing; the art is important. Many times your creativity, or art, helps to distinguish you from your competition. On the other hand, if we value the art and we also value activity, we have no way of accurately measuring Marketing.

This chapter combines art with science. You need both in order to be successful. A great deal of art is involved in creating well-worded, powerful sales messages. Some people are just simply artists with words. Choosing the right marketing activity, promoting it and executing it well also takes a fair degree of art.

The ROI-based Sales and Marketing methodology allows for both the art and the science parts of Marketing. To develop your Sales Cycle, you need to determine the following for *each stage* of the customer's Buying Cycle.

We will step through the Sales Cycle, piece by piece, later on in this chapter.

HOW MARKETING IS TYPICALLY APPROACHED TODAY

From a Sales Message Perspective

We Keep the Same Sales Messages for Everyone

Imagine you have two ducks in a pond, one gun, and one bullet and you are extremely hungry. Where do we normally shoot the gun in Marketing? The answer most often given is, "Right down the middle!"

In normal marketing, we give the same sales messages to all of our customers. But are all of our customers the same? Do they all have the same concerns? Does a financial or business buyer have the same needs/wants as a technical buyer? Should they get the same messages? In most cases, no. Therefore, we must tailor our messages to match the audience.

We Change Sales Messages Frequently

We normally find that companies have a plethora of sales messages. They change messages like people change clothes. They put them on and take them off at a very rapid pace. Perhaps they are tired of them. Perhaps they want something new. Perhaps the politics of the company have changed; hence the messages change with the management team. There are lots of reasons why companies change messages frequently.

Here's the problem with changing messages frequently: It takes time to absorb the messages. If we changes messages like we change clothes, we drive a message-of-the-minute club mentality.

What's the End Result?

Quite frankly, confusion. Salespeople and customers cannot possible keep up with all of the sales messages thrown at them. The result is that salespeople sell what's easy (not necessarily what customers need), and customers buy what they understand (but if they're confused, they may not even take the time to figure out how what you have is important to them).

> IT'S OUR TARGETED SALES MESSAGES—
> DELIVERED THROUGH WELL-EXECUTED,
> FOCUSED SALES AND MARKETING ACTIVITIES—
> THAT *PROPEL* AND *COMPEL* THE CUSTOMER TO
> MOVE FORWARD IN THE BUYING CYCLE.

What's the Solution?

The solution consists in a select few, targeted sales messages aimed directly at the customer and the customer's needs so that we can help the customer move through his or her Buying Cycle as quickly and efficiently as possible.

From a Marketing Mix Perspective

Take a look at the figure "Develop the Sales Cycle to Match the Customer's Buying Cycle" on the next page. Look at the eight steps. Which step do we normally begin with in Marketing?

The answer we usually hear is step 4 (Choose the best sales and marketing activities) although they are not necessarily the best activities, because most companies don't know how to determine what is best) or step 6 (Execute the plan).

If you chose step 1, you are definitely ahead of the game!

Let's look at what happens if you start with step 4 (Choosing the activities) or step 6 (Execute the plan).

Choosing the Activities

Many times companies allocate a certain budget to Marketing. They say to the marketing people, "Here, spend this money as wisely as you can. Don't go over budget. At the end of the year, we'll let you know if you were successful. If Sales makes its numbers, you are successful. If Sales doesn't make its numbers, you are not successful."

Sound familiar?

Okay, now let's examine what marketing people typically do. They are not quite sure how to best spend the money. Should they spend it

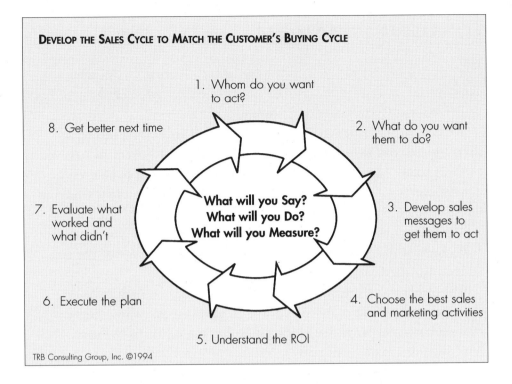

DEVELOP THE SALES CYCLE TO MATCH THE CUSTOMER'S BUYING CYCLE

1. Whom do you want to act?

2. What do you want them to do?

3. Develop sales messages to get them to act

4. Choose the best sales and marketing activities

5. Understand the ROI

6. Execute the plan

7. Evaluate what worked and what didn't

8. Get better next time

**What will you Say?
What will you Do?
What will you Measure?**

TRB Consulting Group, Inc. ©1994

on advertising? direct mail? telemarketing? seminars? road shows? proposal boilerplates? newsletters? (The list goes on and on.)

Marketing people hedge their bets. Since they are not sure which is best, they sprinkle their money here and there: a little in advertising, a little in direct mail, a little in newsletters, and so on. We call this spray-and-pray marketing. They spray the money around and then they pray they will get results! Scary but true!

Going Straight into Execution Mode
Some companies fly by the seat of their pants. They may choose their activities in the beginning of the year in the form of a marketing plan, but as the year proceeds, the "plan" goes by the wayside. "Fire drills" take precedence, and the Marketing and Sales organizations go into activity mode. Remember the Alice-in-Wonderland-and-the-Red-Queen syndrome? ("I'm running as fast as I can, but I don't know where I'm going!")

LET'S CHANGE THE APPROACH!

If we match our Sales Cycle to the customer's Buying Cycle, then we can say and do certain things that will move the customer through his or her Buying Cycle faster and more efficiently.

We must also ensure that we are not saying and doing the same things for all of our products, services or classes of buyers. What we say or do is totally dependent and focused on the prospect profile we have determined for a particular product/service and the customer's Buying Cycle that we have identified.

The following worksheets will help you to determine your selling plan. Be sure to complete these worksheets for *each stage* of the customer's Buying Cycle.

It is important to remember that the activities you choose to do must be cohesive, so that when you add up these activities, they easily move a customer from one stage of the Buying Cycle to the next. We have seen too many instances of Marketing's deciding to do an activity in a vacuum, with no thought as to what should happen to the customer's experience of Marketing's company both before and after that activity.

BE SURE TO PAY
SPECIAL ATTENTION TO:

- What you will say
- What you will do
- What you will measure

to move the customer through the Buying Cycle as quickly and efficiently as possible.

This further points to the awareness-campaign mentality addressed in Part One. When companies focus only on the awareness stage as "Marketing's job," what happens is that Marketing goes into lead-generation mode. Lead generation is good, but focusing only on the awareness stage of the Buying Cycle is bad. Here's what happens.

- Marketing is told to generate leads. ("Don't worry about anything else; just generate leads.")
- Marketing goes into a frenzy to "get names."
- Marketing does whatever it needs to do to get names, and many times these names may not even be qualified.
- Marketing focuses only on the awareness stage of the Buying Cycle and forgets all of the others. (Thus it is not assisting Sales in any other stages, and Sales questions Marketing's value added.)
- Marketing does not measure what has happened to those leads; it just hands them off to Sales (or many times, throws them over the wall to Sales).

Don't forget the measurement part. Remember the radical statement in Chapter 3?

> **IF YOU'RE NOT GOING TO MEASURE YOUR SALES AND MARKETING ACTIVITIES, DON'T BOTHER DOING THEM BECAUSE YOU WON'T KNOW IF YOU'VE SUCCEEDED OR NOT. YOU'RE WASTING YOUR TIME.**

The following worksheets will help you to:

- Develop powerful sales messages (What you will say?).
- Choose the best sales and marketing activities (What you will do?).
- Develop a mini project plan to carry out the effort.
- Determine what your measurement strategy will be (What you will measure?).

SALES AND MARKETING OPERATIONS PLAN
(SALES CYCLE WORKSHEETS)

These worksheets need to be completed for each stage of the customer's Buying Cycle.

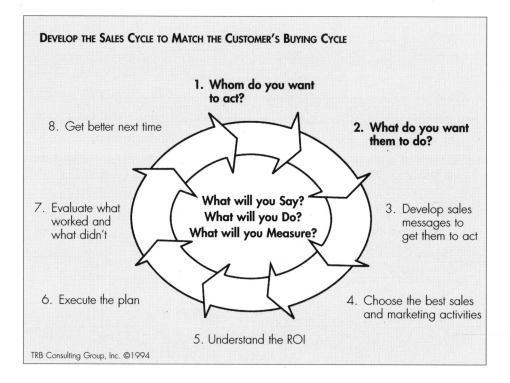

DEVELOP THE SALES CYCLE TO MATCH THE CUSTOMER'S BUYING CYCLE

1. Whom do you want to act?

2. What do you want them to do?

8. Get better next time

What will you Say?
What will you Do?
What will you Measure?

3. Develop sales messages to get them to act

7. Evaluate what worked and what didn't

6. Execute the plan

5. Understand the ROI

4. Choose the best sales and marketing activities

TRB Consulting Group, Inc. ©1994

≋ 1. WHOM DO YOU WANT TO TAKE ACTION? ≋

≋ 2. WHAT DO YOU WANT THEM TO DO? ≋

BUY/SELL CYCLE   Stage _____

Target audience title

_____

_____

_____

_____

_____

_____

Number of people in audience:

_____

(How many are you starting with at this point?)

Actions you want the audience to take to move forward in the
Buying Cycle:

_____

_____

_____

_____

_____

_____

_____

_____

_____

_____

_____

_____

_____

_____

Number of people needed to take this action:

_____

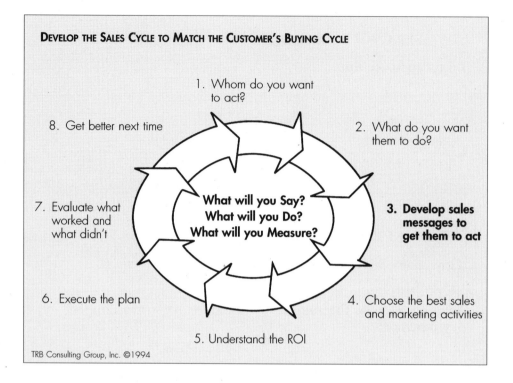

DEVELOP THE SALES CYCLE TO MATCH THE CUSTOMER'S BUYING CYCLE

1. Whom do you want to act?

2. What do you want them to do?

3. Develop sales messages to get them to act

4. Choose the best sales and marketing activities

5. Understand the ROI

6. Execute the plan

7. Evaluate what worked and what didn't

8. Get better next time

What will you Say? What will you Do? What will you Measure?

TRB Consulting Group, Inc. ©1994

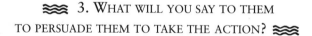

≋ 3. WHAT WILL YOU SAY TO THEM
TO PERSUADE THEM TO TAKE THE ACTION? ≋

Creating Powerful Sales Messages

What can you say that is so powerful, so influential, so motivational that people in your target audience will be propelled and compelled to take action?

For each stage of the Buying Cycle that a customer goes through, there must be a corresponding set of sales messages that are so persuasive and compelling that the target audience is propelled to take the actions that you want it to take.

Imagine you are talking to those in the target audience. What will you say that is so persuasive, compelling, and mind-boggling that they *must* take the desired action?

To develop well-constructed sales messages, consider the following factors when building the strongest sales messages possible.

- How does the audience think?
- Are your sales messages in the customers' language?
- Will customers be able to relate to what you're saying and how you will be able to help them?
- Are your sales messages *complete*? Have you told the whole story?
- Are your sales messages *consistent*? with each other? with other products? with other groups within the company?
- Are your sales messages *believable*?
- Have you differentiated yourself from your competition? Why are you better?
- Is what you are saying important to the customer?

SALES MESSAGES

List the sales messages that will convince your target audience to move forward in the Buying Cycle. Do a first pass. The sales message template that follows should help you to string sales messages that are powerful and persuasive.

_____

_____

_____

_____

_____

_____

_____

_____

_____

_____

_____

_____

_____

_____

Customer Business Environment	Customer Business and Personal Needs	Features/ Characteristics of Your Product	Your Competitive Advantage	Impact on Customer's Business
_____	_____	_____	_____	_____
_____	_____	_____	_____	_____
_____	_____	_____	_____	_____
_____	_____	_____	_____	_____
_____	_____	_____	_____	_____
_____	_____	_____	_____	_____
_____	_____	_____	_____	_____
_____	_____	_____	_____	_____

Ask yourself the following questions while filling out the "Creating Powerful Sales Messages" worksheet.

Customer Business Environment	Customer Business and Personal Needs	Features/ Characteristics of Your Product	Your Competitive Advantage	Impact on Customer's Business
1. What is going on in the customer's business or industry that is driving his or her behavior?	1. What is important to the customer (from both business and personal perspectives)?	1. What characteristics or aspects of your product are important to this customer?	1. What competitive advantage does your product have?	1. What impact will your feature and your competitive advantage have on your customer?
2. Why is the customer feeling pain/ pressure in life or on the job?	2. What keeps the customer awake at night?	2. List only those features that are important.	2. Measure your competitive advantage: • If it is better, how much better? • If it is faster, how much faster?	2. Will it help the customer to: • Increase revenue? • Decrease costs? • Become more productive?
			3. Can you prove this?	3. Can you prove this?

In using this template, string across the page (from Customer Business Environment to Impact on Customer's Business) by filling in each column. The following formula might help you in stringing a sales message.

Due to [Customer's Business Environment], you need to [Customer's Business and Personal Needs]. XYZ Company's [Feature + Competitive Advantage] will enable you to [Impact on Customer's Business].

See XYZ Company's "Sales and Marketing Operations Plan" at the end of this chapter to see an example of the sales message creation template.

Once the analysis of your product is done, usually one of two things happens.

1. You find out that your product is so powerful and the impact on the customer's business is so great that you might increase your revenue targets, increase your prices or expand your markets.
2. You find out that your product is a me-too, with no great advantage or distinction from the competition, so you decide to kill the product.

We have seen both of the above situations result. In the first case, we were working with an artist who decided to double his prices and change his sales and marketing messages and activities to focus more on his target audience than ever before. Success (from a break-even point of view) was predicted to result from three sales, but he made more than twenty!

In another instance of the first case, we worked with a restaurant that decided that its cuisine was unique to its geographic area. The food was excellent; it continually got rave reviews. After using our methodology, the client realized that its prices were too low. It had been comparing itself to the dozens of fast-food and plain-vanilla restaurants in the area. An analysis of its product and the target market revealed it was unique. As a result, it raised its prices, and no one noticed! (Clearly it had been underpricing). In a poor economic climate, this restaurant was ahead of its last year's business while most companies were off 20–30%.

THE BOTTOM LINE IS:

If you don't do the analysis, you'll never know what the *real* impact on the customer is. By the way, if you don't test your assumptions, you may also lose by delivering messages that customers don't believe or don't care about.

In the second case, we have had customers kill whole product lines. The products in question were shown to have no significant impact on the customer, so rather than throw good money after bad, such companies cut their losses and focused on their better-targeted, higher-impact products.

Choosing the Best Sales and Marketing Mix

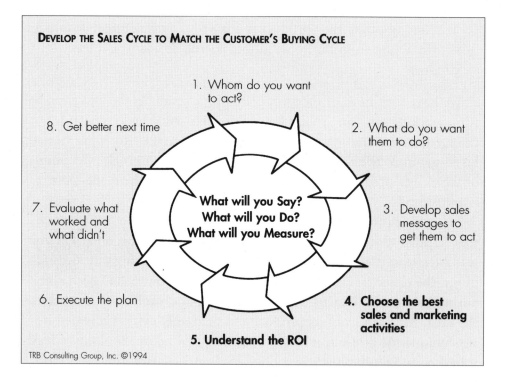

DEVELOP THE SALES CYCLE TO MATCH THE CUSTOMER'S BUYING CYCLE

1. Whom do you want to act?
2. What do you want them to do?
3. Develop sales messages to get them to act
4. **Choose the best sales and marketing activities**
5. **Understand the ROI**
6. Execute the plan
7. Evaluate what worked and what didn't
8. Get better next time

What will you Say?
What will you Do?
What will you Measure?

TRB Consulting Group, Inc. ©1994

〰 4. WHAT WILL YOU DO TO GET THEM TO TAKE THE ACTION? 〰

A sales and marketing activity is a vehicle for transmitting your sales messages to your target customer audience. Examples of sales and marketing activities are:

Advertising	Demos
Trade shows	Newsletters
Direct mail	Telemarketing
Sales/customer training	Brochures
Seminars	Flyers/leaflets
Sales calls	Information sheets

Answers to the following questions influence the selection of the sales and marketing activities.

- How would your sales messages best be received by the target customer audience?
- What are the number of resources needed for each sales and marketing activity? Do you have those resources? Can you gain access to those resources?
- What will be the most effective sales and marketing activity that will influence the target audience? Does the target audience pay attention to the tool you are choosing?

Choose the best Sales and Marketing activities. What is the best combination of sales and marketing activities that you can use to transmit your sales messages? For each sales and marketing activity, ask yourself:

- What is my probability of success? Will I achieve the results I need?
- What is the sales and marketing activity's projected cost?
- What results do I project from using this tool?
- What is my investment per result?*

*Investment per result is calculated by figuring out what the projected results will be from executing a particular sales and marketing activity (how many people will take the desired action) and dividing the projected results by the projected cost of that particular sales and marketing activity. It is important to weigh one sales and marketing activity against another, particularly from an investment-per-result perspective. Many times, what seems like a cost-effective and likely choice is not necessarily the best one.

Sales and Marketing Mix Analysis

List the different ways you can communicate your sales messages to your prospects (trade shows, direct mail, seminars, etc.). Be creative. Once you complete the list, calculate the ROI for each possibility.

Sales and Marketing Activity (trade shows, seminars, etc.)	Quantity Required (No. of people)	No. of People Who Will Act (projected) (C)	Material Prep and Delivery Costs (D)	Total Sales Costs (E)	Total Costs (columns D + E) = (F)	ROI (column F ÷ column C)

(1) The worksheet on the next page can assist in calculating the Total Costs (Column F)
(2) Sales Cost calculation = number of sales calls required (add all sales, tech support, management calls) × avg. cost per call.
Example: 6 calls @ $400/call (loaded average) = $2,400 sales cost

REMEMBER. . .

It is important to evaluate your alternatives *before* you decide the best sales or marketing activity to use.

SALES AND MARKETING MIX COST PROJECTION

Describe the activity/tool (e.g., sales calls, brochures, seminars, direct mail):

_____

Quantity required: _____

Projected results: _____

Estimate the cost of: _____

	Time	$
Preparation	_____	_____
Sales call(s) (1)	_____	_____
Mail	_____	_____
Telephone	_____	_____
Event costs	_____	_____
Facilities	_____	_____
Materials design and creation	_____	_____
Production costs	_____	_____
Advertising costs	_____	_____
Fulfillment	_____	_____
Toll-free number	_____	_____
Business reply card	_____	_____
Materials	_____	_____
Total fulfillment	_____	_____
Other costs	_____	_____
Total cost projection	_____	_____

Total cost projection	_____	(a)
Projected results	_____	(b)
Projected ROI	_____	(a) ÷ (b)

(1) List all calls: sales, tech support, management, etc.

DETERMINE WHAT YOU WILL MEASURE

≋≋ 5. HOW WILL YOU KNOW IF THEY HAVE DONE IT? ≋≋

≋≋ 6. HOW WILL YOU MEASURE IT? ≋≋

You will need to collect data (feedback) in order to determine:

1. If the targeted results have been achieved.
2. The effectiveness of the sales and marketing activity chosen.
3. The effectiveness of the sales message chosen.
   The following information needs to be determined.

- What will be gathered?
- How will it be measured?
- Who will gather the information?
- Number of results achieved
- Actual costs
- Feedback on your sales messages
- Feedback on the sales and marketing activities chosen

To determine what you might want to measure, refer to Chapter 10, "Measuring the Results You Get."

Select the Sales and Marketing Mix

Choose the Sales and Marketing Mix that you believe will be successful. Experiment with new techniques. Determine, in advance, how you will track what is working and what isn't working.

Sales and Marketing Mix	Quantity of Results Required	What Needs to Be Tracked	How	What This Will Tell Me
___	___	___	___	___
___	___	___	___	___
___	___	___	___	___
___	___	___	___	___
___	___	___	___	___

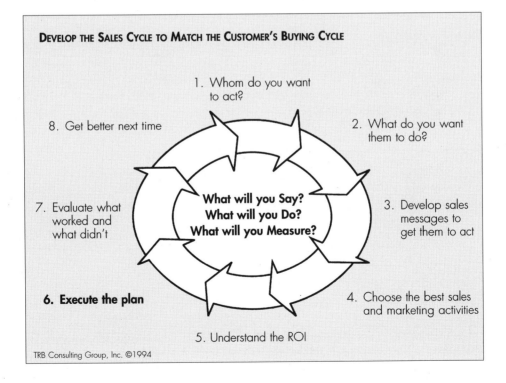

DEVELOP THE SALES CYCLE TO MATCH THE CUSTOMER'S BUYING CYCLE

1. Whom do you want to act?
2. What do you want them to do?
3. Develop sales messages to get them to act
4. Choose the best sales and marketing activities
5. Understand the ROI
6. **Execute the plan**
7. Evaluate what worked and what didn't
8. Get better next time

What will you Say? What will you Do? What will you Measure?

TRB Consulting Group, Inc. ©1994

Carry Out the Effort

This worksheet completes the project planning table and identifies the following factors.

- Actions—which actions need to be taken?
- Time line—how long will it take?
- Due date—when is it due?
- Assignments—by whom?

Actions That Need to Be Taken	How Long Will It Take	When Due	By Whom*

*Note that when any other organization is called upon to take an action, its participation should be mapped out in terms of its role in the customer's Buying Cycle. It would be considered another audience, and as such, its role must be defined. See Chapter 8, "How to Deal with Multiple Audiences," for more information on mapping out multiple audiences.

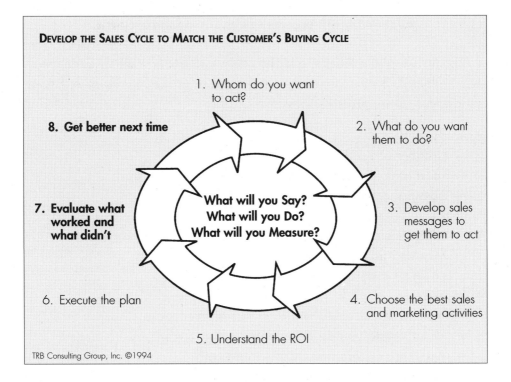

DEVELOP THE SALES CYCLE TO MATCH THE CUSTOMER'S BUYING CYCLE

1. Whom do you want to act?

8. Get better next time

2. What do you want them to do?

What will you Say?
What will you Do?
What will you Measure?

7. Evaluate what worked and what didn't

3. Develop sales messages to get them to act

6. Execute the plan

4. Choose the best sales and marketing activities

5. Understand the ROI

TRB Consulting Group, Inc. ©1994

≈ 5. HOW WILL YOU KNOW IF THEY HAVE DONE IT? ≈

≈ 6. HOW WILL YOU MEASURE IT? ≈

EVALUATION AND IMPROVEMENT

Many people stop after they execute an activity. How will they get better if they don't stop to evaluate what worked, what didn't, and how they can improve next time?

Evaluate: Audience
Sales and marketing mix
Quality of execution
Sales messages
Sales message delivery
ROI

Evaluation is a process of continual improvement.

The last step in a Sales Cycle is to help you *analyze* what you have accomplished, *learn* from the positives and negatives, and *improve* your actions for future projects.

- Analyze
  — Number of results achieved
  — Total cost of each sales and marketing activity
  — Cost per result
- Learn
  — What positive and negative feedback did you get for each:
    •• sales and marketing activity
    •• set of sales messages
- Improve
  With the cost per result and information feedback:
  — What would you do differently?
  — Are there factors beyond your control?
  — How can you implement what you learned?

Evaluation and Improvement Tool

Number of Results Achieved	Total Cost of each Sales and Marketing Mix Selection	Cost per Result	Sales and Marketing Mix +/−	Sales Messages +/−

XYZ COMPANY EXAMPLE: SALES AND MARKETING OPERATIONS PLAN

Example for the Awareness Stage of the Customer's Buying Cycle

BUY/SELL CYCLE   Stage __Awareness__

Target audience title:
___VP of Engineering___

Number of people in audience:
_____5,000_____
(How many are you starting with at this point?)

Action you want the audience to take to move forward in the buying cycle:
___Become aware of the need for widgets___

Number of people needed to take this action:
_____1,000_____

Sales Messages

- Due to shrinking margins, you need to reduce the cost of engineering your products. XYZ's unique design has enabled many of our customers to design their products 20–30% faster.
- This time savings has helped our customers get their products to market faster, thereby giving them a significant edge on their competition and a faster revenue stream.

VP of Engineering's Business Environment	VP of Engineering's Business and Personal Needs	Features/ Characteristics of Our Widgets	Your Competitive Advantage	Impact on Customer's Business
Get products engineered and developed as fast as possible Global competition Shrinking margins Keeping good people	Reduce the cost of engineering a product Reduce the cost of manufacturing a product Get the product to market ASAP Develop products that are easily manufactured Be a hero	Standard design that is easily customizable Extremely cost-effective Highly reliable	Unique—no one else has this. Due to our high up time, dollar for dollar, our widgets have the lowest per unit price (10–20% more effective than our competition). *Proof:* Same article. Most reliable product on market, with a 99.9% up time *Proof:* Article written by *Engineering Times* magazine	Save you time in product design by 20–30% *Proof:* Independent study done by well-known research firm *Proof:* ABC Company saved 15% on overall design time. The savings was worth millions. Save you money in manufacturing downtime *Proof:* ABC Company testimonial

Sales and Marketing Mix Analysis

Sales and Marketing Activity (trade shows, seminars, etc.)	Quantity Required (No. of people)	No. of People Who Will Act (projected) (C)	Material Prep and Delivery Costs (D)	Total Sales Costs (E)	Total Costs (columns D + E) = (F)	ROI (column F ÷ column C)
Response ads placed in engineering trade magazines	1,000	400	$5,000	0	$5,000	$12.50
Direct mail piece (sent to 5,000 VPs of engineering)	1,000	50	$10,000	0	$10,000	$200.00
Telemarketing (phone calls to 1,500 of the 5,000 names)	1,000	300	$9,000	0	$9,000	$30.00
Telemarketing followed by direct mail followed by telemarketing (1,500 initial phone calls/3,500 mail pieces/1,000 follow-up phone calls)	1,000	600	$16,000	0	$16,000	$26.66
Event such as an engineering trade show	1,000	50	$10,000	$1,500	$11,500	$230.00
Executive seminar	1,000	Not applicable for this stage of buying cycle	N/A	N/A	N/A	N/A

Note: The Sales and Marketing activities chosen by XYZ Company are italicized.

Select the Sales and Marketing Mix

Choose the sales and marketing mix that you believe will be successful. Experiment with new techniques. Determine, in advance, how you will track what is working and what isn't working.

Based on the analysis on the previous worksheet, XYZ Company decided to do the following sales and marketing activities.

Sales and Marketing Mix	Quantity of Results Required	What Needs to Be Tracked	How	What This Will Tell Me
Telemarketing/direct mail/telemarketing	600	– # Phoned/ mailed/ phoned – When – # Responses – # Saying no – # Saying not now	Log kept by marketing	• Right quantity? • Out on time? • Success rate • Bad addresses • Interest in the future
Response ads	400	# Responses: • By business reply card • By phone • By fax	Log kept by marketing	• Success rate • Like/dislike/ preferences

Carry Out the Effort

Actions That Need to Be Taken	How Long It Will Take	When Due	By Whom
Decide which magazines to advertise in	3 weeks	9/1	Susan
Design ad	4 weeks	9/10	Susan
Place ad for January edition		10/1	Susan
Buy list for telemarketing/direct mail/telemarketing campaign	2–3 weeks	9/1	Mark
Create mail piece	4–6 weeks	10/1	Sam
Create telemarketing script	2 weeks	10/1	Sam
Design daily log/tracking sheets	1 week	12/1	Joan

KEY LEARNINGS CHECKLIST

☑ It is imperative to do your homework before identifying what you will do (your sales and marketing activities). This means you must:

- Establish your goals to determine what success is (Business Goal Segmentation).
- Profile your ideal prospect (know exactly whom you are selling to).
- Analyze the customer's Buying Cycle.
  — Know how many people are needed at each stage of the Buying Cycle.
  — Know how long it will take a typical customer to move through the Buying Cycle.

☑ Now you are ready to identify your Sales Cycle (what you will say, do and measure to move the customer as quickly and efficiently as possible through the Buying Cycle).

☑ Sales messages *must*:

1. Be targeted. Remember to aim the sales messages at the target audience.
2. Be consistent between all of your organizations (Sales, Marketing and all channels of distribution).
3. Not change frequently or on a whim. Stick with a sales message once you've tested it. Change it as new products are announced or as the competition changes. Do not put on and take off sales messages as you would clothes. The outcome of frequent changes is confusion on the part of the sales force and (even worse) confusion on the part of customers.
4. Be in the customer's language—particularly focused on the impact of your product's features and competitive advantage on the customer's business.

8

How to Deal with Multiple Audiences

Many times you will be marketing to multiple audiences. By this we mean that more than one person may be involved in the buy decision and they will assume different roles. It is very important to map out all the players and their roles. From the customer point of view, you may be marketing to:

- Decision makers
  - Someone who will find the business aspects of your product or service most important
  - Someone who will find the technical aspects of your product or service most important
- Influencers
  - Might be some internal job titles within the customer's company that can influence the decision maker or it might be:
    - •• The press
    - •• Analysts
- Recommenders
  - Some internal job titles within the customer's company (might be a technical evaluation team) whose recommendation is vital to close the sale
- Approvers
  - Many times there are financial people who are not involved in the decision but could very easily veto the purchase if they have not adequately been marketed to.

- Your own internal people
  — Sales
  — Support or service people
  — Other Marketing organizations within your company
  — Engineering
  — Manufacturing

The important thing to note is that you must map out all players involved in the customer's buying cycle. If you do not, you may forget an important person or organization who could seriously delay, postpone or veto your sale.

It is also important to note that you will most probably be asking for resources from other internal organizations within your company. They must be informed of what's in it for them. In other words,

- What kinds of revenues will you be driving?
- When do you need them in the customer's Buying Cycle?
- What is their role?
- What do you want them to say?
- What do you want them to do?

A well-coordinated Sales, Marketing and Support team is like an orchestra. An uncoordinated Sales, Marketing and Support team is also like an orchestra, but one that is badly out of tune.

Imagine an orchestra in which:

- Different instruments play different music.
- Some vital instruments are missing.
- The audience hasn't been told what the performance is about.
- All of the critics show up.
- You may be losing money on every ticket—you don't know.

THIS IS HOW YOUR CUSTOMER MIGHT FEEL

RESULTS OF SALES AND MARKETING "DIS"-INTEGRATION

What happens when Sales and Marketing don't talk to each other?

- Customers get confused.
- Sales and Marketing feel frustrated.
- More time, money and effort than is necessary are spent on activities.
- Your people begin to burn out.

The more you know about who is going to do what, when and how, the easier it will be for you to:

- Focus your resources.
- Rally everyone around common goals.
- Identify resource constraints and alternatives.
- Get everyone involved in the customer's Buying Cycle to give the customer the same sales messages.

HOW TO MAP OUT MULTIPLE AUDIENCES

Okay, let's look at exactly how you map out multiple audiences.

The first question to ask yourself is:

Who exactly in the customer audience must we market to (to ensure the sale)?

- Decision maker?
- Influencer?
- Recommender?
- Approver?

Remember: every time you market to an audience it will cost you time and money, so choose the audiences you must have in order to be successful.

Next ask yourself what resources must be used internally to ensure the sale? If you are requesting resources from organizations outside your own, you will need to map them out.

This is the process of mapping any audience.

STEP	ACTION
1	Determine whom you want to take action.
2	Determine what they *ultimately* will do (buy, recommend the purchase, recommend an evaluation, sell the product or service, install the product, etc.)
3	Look at *what actions they must take* that will lead up to their end action (double-check how these actions support or help the decision maker move up the decision maker's Buying Cycle).
4	Determine *how many* of the multiple audience you ultimately need to support the customer's final action and how many you will need to take action at each stage of *their* Buying Cycle. Work your way backward. Be sure to determine how many you will need to start with. Do you have that many?
5	Determine *how long* it will take these audiences to move through their respective cycles. Does the time they will take affect your customer's Buying Cycle?*

After you have determined their applicable cycles, then:

STEP	ACTION
6	Determine what you will say to move this audience up their cycle.
7	Determine what you will do to move this audience up their cycle.
8	Determine what you will measure to make sure that you were successful.

*We have seen instances in which Marketing had determined that certain groups within its company would be available to help move the customer through the Buying Cycle. Further examination of the situation revealed that the resources in the groups were insufficient to meet the demand. If they used that resource, as planned, they could not have moved the desired number of customers through the Buying Cycle in a timely fashion. The company had to locate alternative resources to fill in the gap.

Examine the various Buy/Sell Cycles that you have created. Also examine the quantities needed and the time it will take. Quite often, several things might come out as a result of this analysis.

- There might be significant resource constraints, and exclusive reliance on those resources would not be effective in moving through the Buying Cycle the numbers of customers that you need
- The amount of time that it would take to get a resource or a channel of distribution up to speed (i.e., learning about a product, signing a contract to be a reseller, etc.) may actually affect the time it would take to move a customer through the Buying Cycle. You may have to think of other creative ways to accomplish the same results by using different methods. We will discuss this further in the next chapter, "Creating Hard-Hitting and On-Target Sales and Marketing Strategies."

Let's look at a generic map of audiences. Then let's look at one for XYZ Company.

Example of Multiple Buy/Sell Cycles

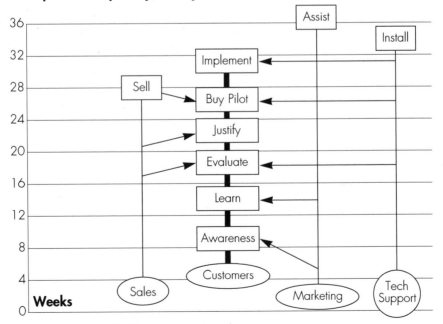

TRB Consulting Group, Inc. ©1994

Remember XYZ's customer's Buying Cycle from Chapter 6? We show it below.

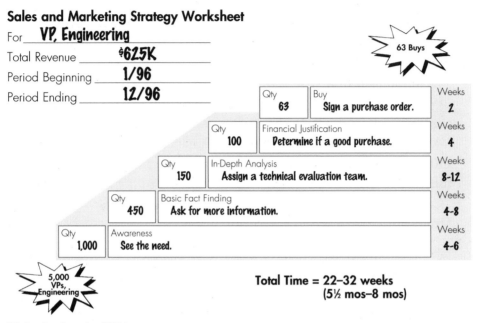

Sales and Marketing Strategy Worksheet

For **VP, Engineering**

Total Revenue **$625K**

Period Beginning **1/96**

Period Ending **12/96**

63 Buys

Qty	Buy	Weeks
63	Sign a purchase order.	2

Qty	Financial Justification	Weeks
100	Determine if a good purchase.	4

Qty	In-Depth Analysis	Weeks
150	Assign a technical evaluation team.	8-12

Qty	Basic Fact Finding	Weeks
450	Ask for more information.	4-8

Qty	Awareness	Weeks
1,000	See the need.	4-6

5,000 VPs, Engineering

Total Time = 22–32 weeks
(5½ mos–8 mos)

TRB Consulting Group, Inc. ©1994

When you are working with multiple audiences, you might want to represent the customer's Buying Cycle in a more linear fashion (see page 125). This linear depiction allows us to view multiple audiences and their Buy/Sell Cycles at once.

XYZ's Multiple Buy/Sell Cycles

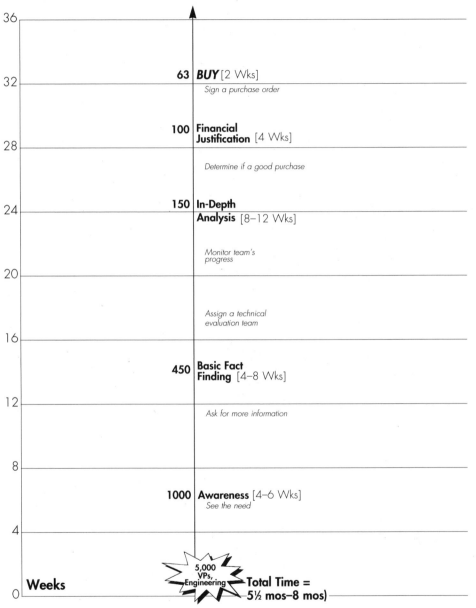

| 36 |
32	**63**	***BUY*** [2 Wks]
		Sign a purchase order
28	**100**	**Financial Justification** [4 Wks]
		Determine if a good purchase
24	**150**	**In-Depth Analysis** [8–12 Wks]
		Monitor team's progress
20
		Assign a technical evaluation team
16
	450	**Basic Fact Finding** [4–8 Wks]
12		*Ask for more information*
8
	1000	**Awareness** [4–6 Wks]
		See the need
4
0	**Weeks**	5,000 VPs, Engineering — **Total Time = 5½ mos–8 mos)**

We can now map the other audiences that will participate in the VP of Engineering's Buying Cycle. For instance, this VP will need to assign a technical evaluation team. Let's look at the technical evaluation team's actions and quantify how many teams we will need in order to be successful.

XYZ's Multiple Buy/Sell Cycles

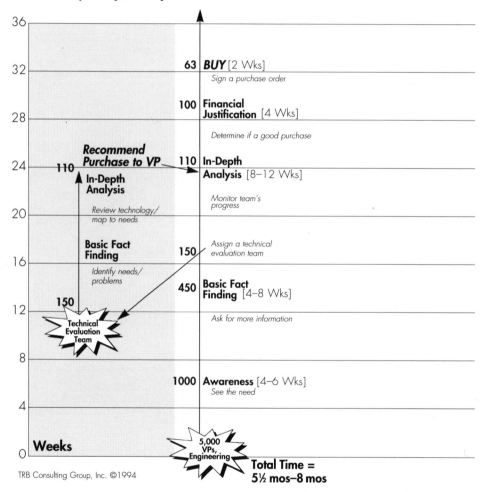

TRB Consulting Group, Inc. ©1994

Notice that XYZ's numbers changed slightly. The company originally thought it needed 150 VPs to go through the In-Depth Analysis stage, but on analysis of its customers, it determined that in actuality it would need 150 technical evaluation teams to start and 110 of those teams to recommend purchase to the VP. So it really needed 110 VPs at the In-Depth Analysis stage. Note that the quantification process is iterative. The important thing to remember when quantifying is to have the right people working on the numbers. By the right people, we mean people who are working with customers every day (i.e., Sales, Support, Marketing, etc.).

We also know that XYZ's sales force will be involved in the customer's Buying Cycle, for it is the channel of distribution that XYZ has chosen to sell to large corporations. Let's look at sales' actions as they relate to the customer's Buying Cycle.

XYZ's Multiple Buy/Sell Cycles

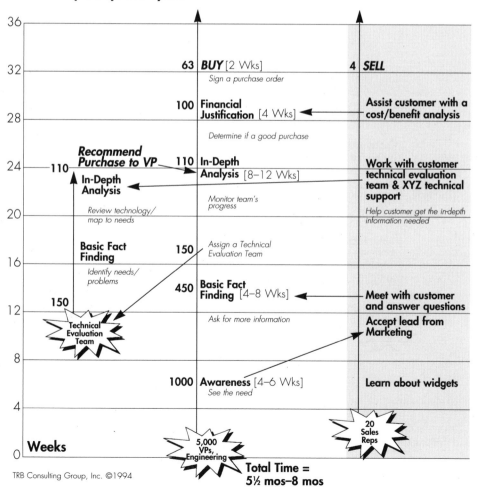

TRB Consulting Group, Inc. ©1994

When you quantify another audience, such as Sales, be sure to ask yourself how many you need to support the customer's final action (in this case, "buy"). In order to have 63 VPs buy XYZ's widgets, how many salespeople will actually be selling/closing those sales? In XYZ's case, four sales reps out of 20 would actually be closing the widget sales.

Also note that if there were other channels of distribution involved in the customer's Buying Cycle (e.g., resellers or distributors), we would simply map in their actions and quantities needed as well.

Now let's look at XYZ's Buy/Sell Cycle for all audiences.

XYZ's Multiple Buy/Sell Cycles

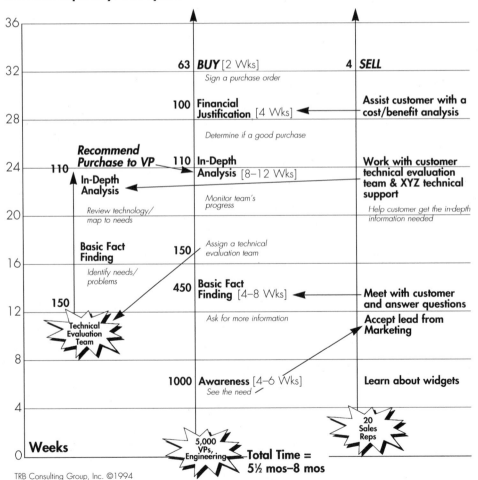

TRB Consulting Group, Inc. ©1994

KEY LEARNINGS CHECKLIST

☑ It is important to identify *all* of the players involved in the customer's Buying Cycle, so that they know their role: when they come in, what is expected of them, what you want them to say, what you want them to do. It is important to get their buy-in before you commit their resources and before you set customer expectations on their involvement.

☑ It is *imperative* that Sales and Marketing act as a cohesive unit. When Sales and Marketing organizations "dis"-integrate:

- Customers get confused.
- Sales and Marketing feel frustrated.
- More time and money are spent than is necessary.
- Everyone in your organization starts to burn out.

9

Creating Hard-Hitting and On-Target Sales and Marketing Strategies

Most people at this point would say, "Great. I've got it. We're done. Right? Let's execute our plan." To this we respond, "You're not totally done yet." So far you've:

- Done a Business Goal Segmentation (so you know where your revenue is coming from and what success is).
- Identified the ideal prospect for your top product.
- Identified the customer's Buying Cycle and quantified it:
  — How many customers are needed at each stage of the Buying Cycle
  — How much time it will take for a customer to move through the Buying Cycle
- Identified your Sales Cycle:
  — What we will say
  — What we will do
  — What we will measure

So, what's missing? Fine tuning—optimizing the plan to ensure your success.

Take a final look at the customer's Buying Cycle and then look at your Sales Cycle (particularly what you will say and what you will do).

- Can you do anything differently that will move the customer through his or her Buying Cycle faster? more efficiently?
- Can you provide the customer with any information sooner so that he or she is better informed and won't need to take the time to discover this information later in the Buying Cycle (when time is more critical)?
- Do you need to change your strategy to better optimize your resources? We had a corporation that before working with us calculated it was spending 39–46 person-days per sale. By going through *The Buck Starts Here*, the client estimated it would need 22½–26½ person-days per sale. On the low side, this is a seven-day savings per sale; on the high side, it is a 20-day savings. Multiply these figures by the cost per person and the number of sales, and the calculation comes out to some very large numbers.
- Do you need to change your organizational structure to make yourselves more customer focused? to make your Sales and Marketing organizations more integrated?

The point here is that you are not done until you fine-tune your plan. You must look at the revenue you will generate and the expenditures you will need to make (in people time and in money) to generate that revenue. You must be sure that the plan will work. You must be sure that you are making a good business decision.

We have had customers who decided after only two or three days of planning not to go into a certain market—that they would lose money on every sale. Was this a good use of their time? Was this a good outcome? You bet it was. It is far better to get out of a market that you will lose money in *before* you go into the market and lose the money!

We have also had customers who discovered that they could make far more money than they originally thought and have increased their forecasts. Their management team was delighted!

Many of our customers have not actually decreased the amount of money they have spent. They have determined that they would spend their money differently. In the past, they had been doing certain marketing activities because it "felt" like a good idea. Upon analysis, using ROI-based Sales and Marketing methodology, they determined they were not getting the best ROI possible. They ultimately changed how they would spend their money.

XYZ Company: Their Completed Sales and Marketing Strategy

Let's go back to XYZ's final U.S. widget plan. Remember that the company needed to generate $625K in the United States in widgets. Ultimately, it thinks it will need to spend $94K in *total* Sales and Marketing expense to generate that revenue. Here is how the firm ultimately decided spend its money.

XYZ's Multiple Buy/Sell Cycles

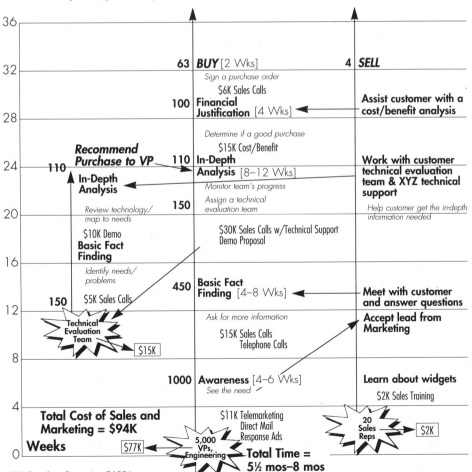

TRB Consulting Group, Inc. ©1994

KEY LEARNINGS CHECKLIST

☑ It is important to refine the customer's Buying Cycle and your Sales Cycle prior to execution. Ask yourself:

- Can you do anything differently to move customers through the Buying Cycle faster?
- Are your chosen sales and marketing activities a flow so that it's easy for the customer to progress from one stage to the next?
- Do your sales messages flow from one stage to the next? Do they deliver impact to the customer at each stage?
- Are you organized properly to move the customer quickly and efficiently through the Buying Cycle?

10

Measuring the Results You Get

Measurement is one of the most important aspects of Marketing for a good ROI, yet it is rarely done in Sales and Marketing. Here are the main reasons why measurement is rarely done:

1. People perceive that measurement is time consuming.
2. People perceive that measurement is difficult and labor intensive.
3. People don't know what to collect.

If measurement is done properly, none of the above is true. In fact, measuring where you stand is not difficult if you know what to measure—nor is it labor intensive or time consuming. It really depends on what you choose to count. Chapter 10 focuses on those items that are easy to count but will provide you with the information you need to determine just where you stand:

- how many customers are at each stage of the Buying Cycle
- how long is it taking the customers to move through the Buying Cycle
- what you will need to adjust in your own Sales Cycle (what you will say or do) to compel more customers to take action and move further up the Buying Cycle

Measurement is the key factor in evaluation and improvement. How can you improve if you don't know where you stand? Furthermore,

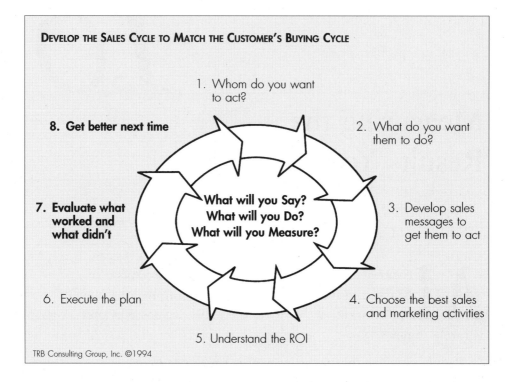

DEVELOP THE SALES CYCLE TO MATCH THE CUSTOMER'S BUYING CYCLE

1. Whom do you want to act?

8. Get better next time

2. What do you want them to do?

What will you Say?
What will you Do?
What will you Measure?

7. Evaluate what worked and what didn't

3. Develop sales messages to get them to act

6. Execute the plan

4. Choose the best sales and marketing activities

5. Understand the ROI

TRB Consulting Group, Inc. ©1994

how can you adjust your Sales and Marketing strategy if you don't know what is or isn't working?

We have talked about matching our Sales Cycle to match the customer's Buying Cycle. Without measurement, there is no way for you to do steps 7 and 8 of the Sales Cycle Development Chart.

Most people find measurement difficult because they have no idea what to measure. They would like to measure marketing's activities on revenue, but most of the time that is impossible. The only times that it is possible to measure a marketing activity directly on revenue is when the vehicle we are employing is used *exclusively* to sell (e.g., a trade show in which the goods are sold directly on the floor or a direct mail catalog or a telemarketing campaign in which we sell directly through that vehicle). In those cases, the vehicles themselves become channels of distribution. Most marketing activities, however, do not fall into the category of a sales vehicle. Most are used to condition the target audience—to move the customer through awareness to buying. In those instances, we must measure the activity on its contribution of moving the customer through the Buying Cycle. We must measure how many customers moved from one stage of the Buying Cycle to the next as a direct result of the activity.

People also find it difficult to measure because they feel it takes too long. We made a statement in the beginning of this book: Measurement should take only 2–5% of the time of the total project. That means that what we measure should be:

1. Well thought out prior to execution.
2. Easy to count/measure.

Now that your ROI-based Sales and Marketing plan is completed and will be implemented for your team, you should begin tracking *each sales and marketing campaign and deliverable* you do. What we mean by this is, each time you or your organization does something, count what results you achieved.

Ask yourself the following questions each time *before* you plan to do an activity.

- Will this sales and marketing activity help accomplish our business objectives?
- What is the result we need? (What do we want people in the target audience to do?)
- How are we going to count whether we're successful or not?

Ask yourself the following questions *after* you have delivered the activity and as you evaluate its success or failure.

- Did this sales and marketing activity help us to accomplish our business objectives?
- What were the results we needed? (What did we want people in the target audience to do?)
- Did we accomplish it? (Did they do it?)
- What did we count to determine whether we were successful or not? Were these the right things to count?
- How did this activity fit with the other activities we did to move the customer forward in his or her Buying Cycle?
- Were we able to move the customer forward as quickly and efficiently as possible?

Make sure that each sales and marketing activity chosen has a measurement capture plan.

- How many people taking action do you need?
- What sales and marketing activity have you chosen?
- What will you count?
- How/By whom?
- What will this tell you?

You have already answered these questions in the Sales Cycle in the following worksheet.

Sales and Marketing Mix	Quantity of Results Required	What Needs to Be Tracked	How	What This Will Tell Me
_____	_____	_____	_____	_____
_____	_____	_____	_____	_____
_____	_____	_____	_____	_____
_____	_____	_____	_____	_____

RECURRING QUESTIONS

Here are some questions you should answer before you begin to execute a particular marketing activity. The results of these questions should be stated in your monthly or quarterly report when the activity is completed. (An example of a reporting template is given in the next chapter.)

Ask these questions for every marketing activity that you do.
- Is this activity planned (vs. unplanned)?
- How many people in your target audience do you need to take action (based on an ROI-based Sales and Marketing plan)?
- How many actually took the action?
- How many eventually took an action based on the objectives you set?

- Did they give you any feedback on the sales messages that you've made about your product/solution or about why they should take action?
- Did you get any feedback about how well the marketing activities you used were delivered?
- What worked? What didn't?
- Did any customers move forward in the Buying Cycle or perhaps jump to the next stage of the Buying Cycle (maybe further along than you expected)? Why? Can you duplicate this?
- How much did the activity cost (in time and/or money)?
- What was the ROI?
- What are creative ways of measuring this (e.g., partnering with third parties).

PHYSICAL ACTION OR FEELING CHANGE?

What does the customer *have* to do in order to buy?

- Ask for more information. (physical action)
- Place an order. (physical action)
- Get questions answered. (physical action)
- Assign an evaluation team. (physical action)
- Conduct a pilot. (physical action)
- Request a proposal. (physical action)
- Become aware. (feeling change)
- See a need. (feeling change)
- Acquire a belief. (feeling change)

When you ask yourself "What must the customer do in order to buy?" look at the actions that you list. Some actions are physical actions ("Ask for more information." "Assign an evaluation team." "Request a proposal."). Physical actions are easy to count. How many "Asked for more information"? How many "Assigned an evaluation team"? Once you know the physical actions a customer must take in order to buy, you can easily count (measure) how many customers took that action.

Now let's look at the other kind of response customers might have—namely, feeling changes. The customer might have to "See a need," "Acquire a belief," "Become aware." Feeling changes are hard to measure. You have one of two ways to measure them.

1. Ask customers if they have acquired a feeling change. For example, if a customer must "Become aware" in order to buy, then when we are measuring our marketing activities, we must ask them, "Have you become aware?" This means that we must survey—and it must be done *before* we do the marketing activity and it must be done *after* to see what the feeling change is. We have to measure the difference. Surveying takes time and money. But, there is another way.
2. See how many customers took a physical action, and assume that the feeling change happened as a result of your marketing. If customers "Ask for additional information," you can safely assume that they have "Become aware" of your product. Therefore, if you market to them to ask for additional information, you can assume that the feeling change of awareness happened as you were marketing to them to ask for additional information.

This does not mean that you can always bypass awareness marketing. It really depends on where you are in the life cycle of your product or your company. If you are brand-new to a market and customers have no knowledge that you are in a particular business, you may very well have to market to awareness. But if you've been in a market for some time and customers know you are in that business, you may not need to market to awareness at all. It really depends on your company, your products and your target audiences.

MEASUREMENT QUESTIONS FOR EACH MARKETING ACTIVITY

Events

Events such as trade shows or customer seminars are the kinds of activities that people like to do. The event itself takes on a life of its own. People feel they are "doing" something. However, when the event is finished and everyone packs up their belongings from the booth, most people say things like, "What did we get out of that event?" and "Why did we do it?"

Many companies focus on events as the end-all-and-be-all of Marketing. We have seen companies in which Marketing's whole purpose is to go from one event to the next. Measurement is never done. Marketing's role is focused at the awareness stage of the customer's Buying Cycle, and Marketing never gets out of that stage. It is in a never-ending awareness loop, and Marketing has no idea if what it is doing has made any contribution toward the customer's purchase. Intuitively, those in Marketing believe that what they are doing has value, but they cannot prove it.

As we mentioned earlier in this chapter, we must measure the movement of the customer through the Buying Cycle. Many companies hold events, such as trade shows, for leads. Doing a trade show for leads is worthwhile if you know the following information.

1. How do you know that these are *real* leads?
2. What is the ROI of your investment per lead, and could you have gotten a better ROI from another marketing activity?

How Do You Know They Are Real Leads?
The biggest no-no in doing an event is to measure leads by using the fishbowl approach. Many companies do this and it's deadly. Here's how it goes. We go to the event (let's say it's a trade show) to generate leads. We get out a giant fishbowl and put out a big sign saying, "WIN A TRIP TO BERMUDA." We have people put their business cards into the fishbowl to win the trip to Bermuda. After all is said and done, when we go back to the office, guess what happens to the business cards? They get delivered to the salespeople as leads and they get put on the corporate database for further marketing activities (such as mailings). Here's what the end results of the fishbowl are.

1. Sales now has further reason not to trust or believe Marketing. (All that the salespeople need to do is make two phone calls to find out that the "leads" they received were really a raffle ticket to go to Bermuda.) Sales will further come to the opinion that Marketing

really doesn't understand what Sales does. Furthermore, Sales will question the value added of Marketing.

2. Those "leads" become a real bottom-line corporate expense. By putting the unqualified "leads" on the corporate database as a true lead (which will receive more corporate marketing materials), the cost of the unqualified lead goes beyond wasting the time of the sales force to actually spending real money on people who just wanted a free vacation.

What Is Your Investment per Lead?

We were working with a client whose marketing organization was committed to doing a particular trade show.

We asked, "Why do you want to do this trade show? What will you get out of it?"

The reply was, "Leads. We'll get leads."

Of course we asked the next logical question: "How many qualified leads do you think you will get out of this trade show?"

The response was, "We'll get five really solid leads."

We then asked, "How much will it cost you to go to this trade show?"

The response was, "$50,000."

Therefore their investment per lead is $10,000 per name. The cost of the entire product was $50,000. Needless to say, this organization took a look at this trade show expense and decided to invest its money in a different marketing activity.

Event Measurement Questions

- Is this a planned event? Why are you doing it?
- How many people in your target audience do you need to attend (based on an ROI-based Sales and Marketing plan)?
- How many actually attended?
- Did they give you any feedback on the sales messages you've made about your product/solution or about why they should take the desired action?
- Did they give you any feedback about the marketing activities you used?

- What worked? What didn't?
- Did any of them move further along the Buying Cycle than you expected? Why?
- How much did the event cost?
- What was your cost per person who attended?
- What was the cost per person who did what you wanted them to do (cost per result)?
- If you got leads, are they *real leads* or just names? Are they qualified? How do you know they are qualified? What is the cost per qualified lead (total cost divided by number of qualified leads)?

Direct Mail/Telemarketing

As we mentioned earlier, you can measure direct mail and telemarketing directly on revenue if you are using those vehicles as a sales channel. Many times, however, direct mail and telemarketing are used by companies at all stages of the customer's Buying Cycle to move the customer to the next stage.

Direct Mail

We have seen many direct mail pieces whose materials did *not*:

- Have a call to action.
- Have easy reply mechanisms for the customer to respond.
- Have a readable, easy format for customers to understand the sales messages.

Be sure when doing direct mail pieces that you test the pieces with your sales force and with your customers to make sure that the pieces:

- Are important to the customer.
- Are catchy enough so that the customer will read them and not throw them away.
- Have understandable sales messages that are important to customers so that customers clearly understand the benefit to them of taking the desired action.

- Have response mechanisms that this target audience likes to use (e.g, business reply cards, phone responses, 800-number responses, fax responses, electronic responses).

Telemarketing

We can't tell you how many times we have seen marketing people begin a telemarketing campaign *without*:

- Creating a concise and well-thought-out script for the telemarketing people to follow.
- Creating powerful and persuasive sales messages.
- Training the telemarketing people on the product so that if a customer asks a question outside the script, the telemarketing person knows how to respond.

Direct Mail/Telemarketing Questions

- Who was the target audience you mailed to or phoned?
- What was the desired result (what did you want them to do)?
- How many of them did it (took the desired action)?
- By the way, how did you count this?
  — In the case of direct mail, by business reply cards, or by 800-number responses? by faxes? Which was more effective (i.e., which did people choose to use more)?
- In the case of telemarketing, by actual verbal responses?
- How much did it cost in total?
- For direct mail, how much did each piece cost (total cost divided by number of pieces sent)?
- What was your cost per result (total cost divided by the number of people taking the desired action)?
- What did they say about your sales messages: positive or negative?
- What feedback did you get about your marketing activities?
- What percentage of bad addresses did you have?*

---

*Many companies in the United States consider 10% bad addresses to be acceptable. Because so many people and businesses in the United States are constantly moving, it is vital to purchase lists that are updated frequently.

Customer/Sales Training

Many companies view training as an expense or even a revenue-producing activity, but they are not always clear on how to measure it. The main questions on training are:

- How many people did you need to get trained?
- How many actually got trained?
- Did you use the training to collect other information from your customer or your sales force?

We have seen situations in which some of our clients used training to evaluate:

- How important their sales messages are to their customers.
- Customers' perceptions of certain marketing materials.
- How important the training itself is to customers.

We had one marketing manager who decided that he would measure his success on the attendance ratio of the customers to his training. He wanted to be sure that when he ran a training, 75% of the available slots were taken by customers. This would indicate the importance of the training to his customers.

Customer/Sales Training Questions

- Based on your ROI-based Sales and Marketing plan, how much of your target audience did you need to get trained?
- How many actually got trained?
- What did they say about your sales messages (your solution): positive or negative?
- What did they say about the way you delivered this activity?
- What was the total cost?
- What was the cost per result (total cost divided by the number of people who attended the training)?
- Did you use a measurement tool to measure the training and get feedback?
- If you did, what was the overall rating of the class? How about each session?

- Did you get an attendance ratio to be equal to or greater than 75% of the available slots? (This is a goal and might indicate the importance of the training to the attendees.)
- You might want to consider doing a pre- and post-evaluation survey of the training attendees to test the importance of the sales messages points (your solution) that you are highlighting as well as to test any feeling changes that might have occurred during the training.
- Is this training appropriate for all audiences (e.g., international)?*

Advertising

Advertising falls in line with the physical action/feeling change discussion that we had earlier in this chapter.

Image advertising goes after the feeling changes. We see image ads mostly on TV, in magazines or newspapers, on billboards. These ads have no call to action in them. They generally make customers aware that a company has a particular product or service to offer. Image ads are very hard to measure: just ask someone on Madison Avenue who will answer you truthfully. They entail surveying. As we discussed earlier in this chapter, you must survey a sample population of the target audience prior to the ad to determine their level of awareness of your company or product. You must then market to them through the ad. Then you must survey them again to determine the level of feeling change. By the way, it is very rare to be effective with just one ad. The average customer says no five times before saying yes. Hence, you must run the ad a few times to get results.

Response advertising does just that. You are definitely marketing to customers to make them aware, but you have built in a call to action in your materials. You are trying to get the customer to respond to you by, say, calling a certain phone number or mailing a business reply card

---

*In the case of international companies, we have seen many instances in which corporate does not provide training that is appropriate for all countries. Many times the countries themselves must reinvent the wheel by creating the core training that could have been created by corporate Marketing and then tailored by the individual countries. We call this the cookie-cutter approach. (When you use a cookie cutter, you cut out the cookies and then change each one as you desire: one might have sprinkles, another nuts, another candies, etc.) This can be used in many places in Marketing, where corporate creates the basic template and then the individual geographies, business units, and so on, tailor these materials for their specific, target audiences.

that is part of the ad. The point here is that by having potential customers take a physical action ("Ask for more information"), you can assume that they have "Become aware" of your product or company.

We encourage our clients to look very closely at their advertising spending. We ask them, "What do you want the customer to do?" If they say, "Be a lead," then it is mandatory to use a response ad with a very specific call to action (like call or fax to a specific phone number). "Call your local XYZ Company office" does not qualify as a good call to action, for you will never know if the customer responded.

Response Advertising Questions
- How many people do you want to respond?
- How many actually responded (via a business reply card or a toll-free number)?
- Did you get any additional information about your sales messages?
- What was your total cost to place the ad?
- What was your cost per result (total cost divided by the number of people responding)?
- How many *qualified leads* resulted?
- How do you know they're qualified?
- What was the cost per lead (total cost divided by the number of qualified leads)?

Demonstrations

Demonstrations can be very powerful tools to move the customer through the Buying Cycle. The old adage "Seeing is believing" is true if the customer needs to see the product in order to buy. We have seen many instances in which demos are done for the sake of having a demo. We have been involved with companies that have built demo units used for one event (say, a trade show) and that were never used again. We have seen situations where the company focused all of its efforts to get the customer to gain in-depth information through the use of a demo but only two people in the entire company were qualified to give that demo. As you can imagine, this could totally blow a company's ability to move customers through the Buying Cycle quickly and efficiently.

Demonstration Questions
- Who is the target audience?
- What do you want the demo to show?
- Does it show this?
- What have customers/field reps who have seen the demo say about it?
- What is the total cost of the demo?
- What is its life cycle?
- What is the cost over its life cycle (total cost divided by length of life cycle)?
- Does it have multiple uses?
- When appropriate, measure the number of qualified leads that have resulted as a direct result of the viewing of this demo.
- Could this demo become a prototype of a real, salable and profitable solution? (Might measure the importance/value of the demo.)
- What would happen if we didn't do a demo?
- Are people trained to give the demo?
- Is this demo appropriate for all of your target audiences: domestic as well as international?

Press Events

We have seen situations where a company has decided to hold a press event but the press that appeals to target customers did not attend. Be sure in holding a press event that you invite the press that your target audience reads. And remember: The press could be different for your various products or product lines. You are most probably not always marketing to the same target audience.

One of our customers decided to measure press events on the number of articles that could be used for other purposes, such as reprints.

Press Event Questions
- How many attendees do you want to attend?
- How many attended?
- How many positive articles do you want published?
- How many actually were published?
- How many negative articles were published?

- How many neutral articles were published?
- What is the total cost of holding this event?
- What is the cost per attendee?
- What is the cost per positive article (total cost divided by the number of positive articles published)?
- How many of the articles can be used for other purposes (e.g., reprints/collateral materials)?
- Were the articles in the correct press media to reach your target audience?

Collateral Materials/Sales Tools/Literature/ Presentation Materials

The first thing that companies usually produce is a brochure or an info sheet. We can't tell you how many times we have seen literature that was not aimed at the target audience—pieces that were so broad in message and scope that they did not target anyone. We encourage you to test your pieces prior to publication. The best ones to test them on are your sales force and actual customers. This can be done through focus groups (usually a one-shot deal where you bring your target audience into a session and test their reactions to your messages or your materials) or through advisory boards* (usually ongoing sessions with customers to determine their needs as your product/service evolves).

Collateral Materials/Sales Tools/Literature/Presentation Materials Questions

- What is the total cost of production?
- What is the cost per piece?
- What did the receivers of these materials say about your sales messages: positive or negative?
- Did you build in a call to action? If so, did those in the audience do it?
- Did you measure that they took the desired action?
- How many additional requests have you received for these materials? (Might indicate demand.)
- What went right/wrong about the delivery vehicle you chose to present the desired information?
- Is/are your content/sales messages correct?

*In many companies strategic advisory boards are used from a product engineering point of view. Customers are requested to attend several sessions on an ongoing basis so that the company can determine if it should change the product (usually from a technical point of view). Most companies do not use already existing advisory boards to evaluate their marketing messages and materials. We suggest that if you already have an existing advisory board for a particular product, you should consider asking your customers to assist you by telling you:

- Why they bought the product
- What the product has done to impact their business
- What publications they read
- What their reaction is to your sales messages
- What their reaction is to your marketing materials (ad mock-ups, direct mail piece layouts, etc.)

You would be surprised how much your customers want to help you.

Field/Customer Communications

Many companies publish newsletters for their customers or sales force. Such a publication generally acts like a constant stream of information out with no input in as to whether or not anyone out there is listening. We had one client who had been sending out a very expensive magazine to customers for years. The company had not tested or verified the list for a long time. After working with us, the firm discovered that some of the subscribers on its list were dead.

If your company is doing the same thing, we suggest that you build a call to action into your newsletter by offering something to your customers that gets them to respond. It could be an offer for additional information (and by the way, responses to this can be considered leads); it could be a please-resubscribe request so that you know customers are interested in continuing to receive the publication; it could be a survey.

Remember the fishbowl we talked about earlier? Names from fishbowls usually end up in the newsletter database. So, if your company publishes an expensive magazine like the company cited here, think about how much money you're wasting on fishbowl names that go into the corporate database and that are ultimately destined to receive ongoing communications. The old adage "If you watch your pennies, the dollars usually take care of themselves" definitely applies here. The fishbowl has long-reaching aftereffects.

Field/Customer Communications Questions
- How many subscribers have you received to date?
- Is this an increase or a decrease (over time)?
- What have the subscribers said about your sales messages? (You might want to do a survey to get this feedback.) Test your sales messages on content as well as the format of the information presented.
- What is the total cost to produce this? (Don't forget people time.)
- What is the cost per edition?
- What is the cost per subscriber (total cost divided by number of editions divided by number of subscribers)?
- How many people respond to you when you request information? (Might indicate interest/value to the subscribers.)
- Are your sales messages appropriate for your audience (i.e., domestic and international)?

KEY LEARNINGS CHECKLIST

Remember our radical statement in Chapter 3?

> **IF YOU'RE NOT GOING TO MEASURE YOUR SALES AND MARKETING ACTIVITIES, DON'T BOTHER DOING THEM BECAUSE YOU WON'T KNOW IF YOU'VE SUCCEEDED OR NOT. YOU'RE WASTING YOUR TIME.**

Without measurement, you have no way of knowing if you are on or off target. You will revert to spray-and-pray mode in sheer panic.

☑ Make sure that each activity chosen:

1. Will help you to achieve your business objectives.
2. Is measurable.
3. Has a measurement plan (what you will count, who will do it, how will they do it, what this will tell you).

☑ If you have chosen some activities that are aimed at customer feeling changes (acquire a belief, see a need, become aware), make sure you have a measurement plan in place to see if the feeling change has taken place. This can take the form of:

1. A survey taken before and after the sales and marketing activities to determine if the feeling change took place.
2. Measuring customers' physical actions.

11

Reporting
Your Results

One of the biggest fears people suffer from is having to report "bad" results. No one wants to be the deliverer of bad news. They are afraid of repercussions (from a business perspective, no more funding; from a personal perspective, bad reviews or less money). We as managers have conditioned employees to tell us only the good news—and that is exactly what we get. This does not imply that we always get the truth; we get what we ask for.

ROI-based Sales and Marketing asks Management to change those views. Find out what's really going on. Know how customers feel. Be aware of how many customers are acting (moving through the Buying Cycle). Know what has worked and what hasn't worked so that your organization can act out of knowledge—not out of gut feel. In other words, hold people accountable to report their findings. And if the findings aren't great, take action to correct them instead of shooting the messenger.

One of the most important aspects of ROI-based Sales and Marketing is for people who use it to take corrective action in real-time mode. This means that as your organization is implementing a particular activity, you *must* collect the results as the activity is going on. It also means that the reporting of the results is vital in order to make management decisions, such as:

- Should we continue with our current strategy?
- Should we continue to invest in this campaign?
- Should we invest more money than we had originally planned?
- Should we change our sales messages?
- Should we change our target audience?

There is no way to know the answers to these questions without having vital information regarding where your customers currently are in their Buying Cycle and what they are saying about your product/service.

The idea of reporting and of being accountable must become ingrained into the corporate culture from the highest levels.

Through the use of ROI-based-Sales and Marketing reporting templates, which we will discuss shortly, you will be able to answer the above questions. The reporting that will take place in your organizations will be on the movement of your customer through the Buying Cycle. By focusing your reporting on the customer, you will be able to make decisions about increasing/decreasing spending, changing sales messages, focusing on a different target audience, and so forth.

There is another benefit from reporting the measurement of customers through their Buying Cycle. You can have accurate forecasts from your sales force.

Most of the time, sales forecasts are anyone's best guess. However, if you look at the movement of the customer through the Buying Cycle, you can estimate the probability of close for a customer at any stage of the Buying Cycle. You will gain this knowledge of the probability of close from your sales managers (who probably can estimate this now), or, in the case of a new product, you can gather data on the first customers through the Buying Cycle to see if there are any trends.

Following is a blank reporting template for your Marketing and Sales organizations. We have completed a template for the XYZ Marketing Team as well as for an XYZ sales rep—John Smith—as an example.

Marketing Report Template

Marketing Team _____

Target Customer _____

Stages of Buying Cycle	Sales Messages	Sales and Marketing Activities Executed	Measurements Used	Results Achieved (target/actual)	Investment (target: total per actual: total per)
Awareness					
Basic fact finding					
In-depth analysis					
Financial justification					
Buy					
Implement					

Date:

Marketing Report Template

Marketing Team   Widgets

Target Customer   VPs of Engineering >$100M in Sales; >50 Manufacturing Plants

Stages of Buying Cycle	Sales Messages	Sales and Marketing Activities Executed	Measurements Used	Results Achieved (target/actual)	Investment (target: total per / actual: total per)
Awareness	• Reduce the cost of engineering • Design products faster.	Ads Telemarketing Direct mail Telemarketing	# responses # business reply cards, faxes, phone	(400/350) (600/700)	$5,000/$12.50 $6,000/$17.14 $16,000/$26.66 $17,500/$25
Basic fact finding	• Same as awareness	Seminars	# attending	(450/500)	$25,000/$55.56 $27,500/$55
In-depth analysis	• Save 10–20% in production due to our lowest per unit price. • Most reliable product on the market: 99.9% uptime	Sales calls	# completed	(150/75)	$75,000/$500 $45,000/$600
Financial justification	• Specific cost/benefit analysis for each customer	Cost/benefit analysis Sales calls	# requested vs. # completed	(100/25)	$75,000/$750 $25,000/$1000
Buy		Sales calls	# orders	(63/2)	$10,000/$158.73 $400.00/$200
Implement		Support calls	# references	(5/0)	

Date: 5/31/96

Sales Forecast Model Template

Salesperson _____

Account	Proposed Product	Become Aware (0%)*	Gain Initial Info (25%)	Gain In-Depth (50%)	Justify Internally (75%)	Buy (100%)	Revenue Opportunity	Factored Forecast $**
Total							$	$

*Probability %.
**Factored forecast amount = total revenue opportunity × probability %.

December 1996 Forecast

Salesperson _John Smith, Metro North_

Account	Proposed Product	Request Info — Become Aware (0%)*	Complete Needs Analysis — Gain Initial Info (25%)	Request Proposal — Gain In-Depth (50%)	Do a Financial Justification — Justify Internally (75%)	Sign PO — Buy (100%)	Revenue Opportunity	Factored Forecast $**
El Jay Jrs	7715		7/1/96	8/12/96	9/6/96	Projected to close in December	$250K	$187.5K
Dawn Joy	7740	9/15/96	10/15/96	11/1/96		Projected to close in December	$300K	$150K
Bon Jour	7220		10/22/96				$1M	$250K
							$1.55M	$587.5K

* Probability %.
** Factored forecast amount = total revenue opportunity × probability %.

KEY LEARNINGS CHECKLIST

☑ Results should be reported by:

- Marketing
- Sales
- All channels of distribution

☑ The results will tell you where you are:

- On target
- Off target
- By how much

☑ By having sales forecast against the customer's Buying Cycle, you will be able to more accurately forecast your true potential results.

12

Measuring/Managing Your Resources

You have a challenge. You need to manage the investment of your resources (your people, your money, your organization's time) to optimize achieving your business goals. The best way to do this is to focus on the *results* of your investments instead of your activities.

It is the responsibility of everyone in your organization to manage their individual resources. Everyone needs to focus on the customer and the customer's actions. Everyone in your company represents you to the customer. Everything you do represents you to a customer (down to the smallest info sheet and brochure). Everything anyone in your organizations says or does represents your company to your customer.

With that in mind, everyone in the company must learn to manage resources (time, money and people)—even if the resource is only themselves.

To manage your resources effectively, you need to change behavior

- From an *internal* focus to an *external* customer focus
- From *activities* carried out to *results* achieved
- From *spending* the budget to *investing* to achieve results
- From *talking* features to *persuading* customers to take action
- From *rewarding activity* to *rewarding results*
- From *"We-Them"* to . . . *"OUR TEAM"*

As you have seen in *The Buck Starts Here*, we have shown you a logical, commonsense, business focused approach to creating, implementing and measuring your business plan. Now let's talk about how you manage all of your resources from an ROI point of view.

MANAGING YOUR DAY-TO-DAY ACTIVITIES

In order to be successful with this methodology, you need to manage your business from an ROI perspective every day. As you implement your business plan, focus yourself and your people on the following two things:

- Business Results = Revenue/Profit
- Marketing and Sales Results = Movement of the Customer through the Buying Cycle

THE TOOLS AND CHECKLISTS NEED TO MANAGE FROM AN ROI PERSPECTIVE

You have already received most of the tools you will need to manage from an ROI perspective. In this chapter, we will also provide you with checklists for each section. Let's review each of the sections of *The Buck Starts Here* and an associated checklist for you to make sure you're on track.

Sections of The Buck Starts Here

- Business Goal Segmentation (set your business goals)
- Create your customer's Buying Cycle
- Match your Sales Cycle to the customer's Buying Cycle
- Achieve and improve sales and marketing results
- Measure your progress and make adjustments
- Manage yourself and others from an ROI perspective

Business Goal Segmentation Tool

Product ___	Geography ___	Geography ___	Total Revenue
Industry:	$ ___ ___ % Avg. Sale Price = $ ___ # of Sales Needed = ___	$ ___ ___ % Avg. Sale Price = $ ___ # of Sales Needed = ___	$ ___ ___ %
Industry:	$ ___ ___ % Avg. Sale Price = $ ___ # of Sales Needed = ___	$ ___ ___ % Avg. Sale Price = $ ___ # of Sales Needed = ___	$ ___ ___ %

Product ___	Geography ___	Geography ___	Total Revenue
Class of buyer:	$ ___ ___ % Avg. Sale Price = $ ___ # of Sales Needed = ___	$ ___ ___ % Avg. Sale Price = $ ___ # of Sales Needed = ___	$ ___ ___ %
Class of buyer:	$ ___ ___ % Avg. Sale Price = $ ___ # of Sales Needed = ___	$ ___ ___ % Avg. Sale Price = $ ___ # of Sales Needed = ___	$ ___ ___ %

Product _____	Geography _____	Geography _____	Total Revenue
Channel of distribution:	$ _____ _____ % Avg. Sale Price = $ _____ # of Sales Needed = _____	$ _____ _____ % Avg. Sale Price = $ _____ # of Sales Needed = _____	$ _____ _____ %
Channel of distribution:	$ _____ _____ % Avg. Sale Price = $ _____ # of Sales Needed = _____	$ _____ _____ % Avg. Sale Price = $ _____ # of Sales Needed = _____	$ _____ _____ %

Business Goal Segmentation Checklist (Quarterly)

- Are your goals clearly defined in all of the key dimensions?
  — Geography
  — Product
  — Industry
  — Channels of distribution
  — Class of buyer
- Are the business goals challenging and attainable?
- Do you have agreement on the goals from key players?
- Are the business goals supported by the customer Buying Cycle models?
- Do the customer Buying Cycle models show that your goals are attainable? too low? too high?
- Will the overall business plan be achieved by the sum of the individual customer Buying Cycle models?

Create Your Customer's Buying Cycle Tool

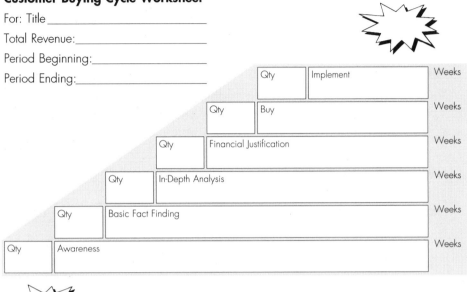

Customer Buying Cycle Worksheet

For: Title _____

Total Revenue: _____

Period Beginning: _____

Period Ending: _____

Qty	Implement	Weeks
Qty	Buy	Weeks
Qty	Financial Justification	Weeks
Qty	In-Depth Analysis	Weeks
Qty	Basic Fact Finding	Weeks
Qty	Awareness	Weeks

TRB Consulting Group, Inc. ©1994

Customer Buying Cycle Checklist
(whenever a customer Buying Cycle model is created)

- Do you know your target audience clearly enough?
- Do you know what role they typically play (decision maker, influencer, recommender, approver)?
- Are you clear about your short-term and long-term goals?
- Do you understand what actions the customer must take in order to reach the short-term and long-term goals?
- Are there clear targets of quantities of results and elapsed time?
- Can you consolidate/collapse some of the stages of the customer's Buying Cycle?

- Can you consolidate this customer's Buying Cycle with others that you have created?
- If there are multiple audiences involved in this customer's Buying Cycle, have you mapped them out?
- Before you begin investment, implementation and execution, is it clear who the team is to drive this plan?
- Have you identified the team leader?
- What is the total investment in this Buying Cycle? (This is derived by adding up all of the Sales and Marketing Activities identified.)
- Does the investment in this Buying Cycle make sense compared with the investment in other Buying Cycles?
- Should you invest in this particular plan?

Match Your Sales Cycle to the Customer's Buying Cycle Tool

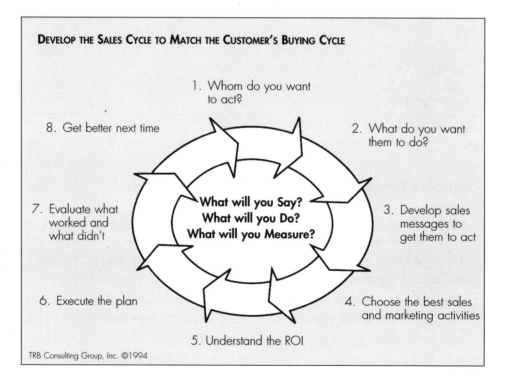

DEVELOP THE SALES CYCLE TO MATCH THE CUSTOMER'S BUYING CYCLE

1. Whom do you want to act?
2. What do you want them to do?
3. Develop sales messages to get them to act
4. Choose the best sales and marketing activities
5. Understand the ROI
6. Execute the plan
7. Evaluate what worked and what didn't
8. Get better next time

What will you Say? What will you Do? What will you Measure?

TRB Consulting Group, Inc. ©1994

Match Your Sales Cycle to the Customer's Buying Cycle Checklist
(whenever a Sales Cycle is created)

- What is the total investment to achieve the customer's Buying Cycle plan?
- Has a Sales Cycle been done for each stage of the customer's Buying Cycle?
- How compelling are the sales messages?
- How complete are the sales messages?
  — Customer's business environment?
  — Customer's business and personal needs?
  — Your competitive advantages?
  — The impact of your product on the customer's business?
- How confident are you that the sales and marketing activities that you have chosen will deliver the expected results?
- What is the expected investment per result?
- Is the expected investment per result approximately the same, much lower or much higher than your past experience has shown you?
- Have you identified what you will collect (measure) including:
  — Did you achieve the desired result?
  — What did the customers say about your sales messages?
  — What went right or wrong with the delivery of your sales and marketing activities?
- Are you clear on how you will collect your results?
- Are the necessary procedures and resources in place to effectively and accurately collect the results?
- Do you have the necessary resources to carry out the effort according to schedule?

Achieve and Improve Sales and Marketing Results—Investment Evaluation Tool

Sales and Market- ing Mix	Stage of Buying Cycle Targeted	Quantity of Results Required	Total Invest- ment	Invest- ment per Result	Perceived Risk	Perceived Strategic Value	Rank in Terms of Impor- tance

Achieve and Improve Sales and Marketing Results—Investment Evaluation Checklist
(whenever an investment is considered)

- Is this a tactical or a strategic investment?
- What is the total investment to achieve the customer Buying Cycle?
- Can you consolidate some/all of the stages of the customer's Buying Cycle?
- Is the customer Buying Cycle for the proposed investment clear, complete, and credible, including target quantities and elapsed times?
- Are the Sales Cycles complete for each stage of the customer's Buying Cycle?
- Does the investment in this customer Buying Cycle make sense compared with other customer Buying Cycles in the company?
- Should you invest to get the results proposed?

Evaluation and Improvement Tool

Number of Results Achieved	Total Cost of each Sales and Marketing Mix Selection	Cost per Result	Sales and Marketing Mix +/–	Sales Messages +/–

Evaluation and Improvement Checklist

- Is it clear who will be responsible for collecting the evaluation and improvement information?
- Is it clear how this information will be transmitted to the rest of the team?
- Have you shared this information with other groups in the company that need to know it?

Measure Your Progress and Make Adjustments—Reporting Template Tools

It is extremely important that your Sales and Marketing people report back monthly (at the least) on their effectiveness in moving the customer through his or her Buying Cycle. It is your responsibility as a manager to work with your people to take additional actions or make strategy adjustments. The additional actions you choose to do or the strategy adjustments you choose to make are dependent on the *results* that you have received from your Sales and Marketing people's activities. If they do not report regularly, you will not have enough information to make an informed decision on the additional actions or strategy changes you might need to make. Therefore, the submission of the reports on the next two pages by both your Sales and your Marketing people are vital to ensure that you know where you stand at all times.

Marketing Report Template

Marketing Team _____

Target Customer _____

Stages of Buying Cycle	Sales Messages	Sales & Marketing Activities Executed	Measurements Used	Results Achieved (targeted/actual)	Investment (Targeted: total/per; actual: total/per)
Awareness					
Basic fact finding					
In-depth analysis					
Financial justification					
Buy					
Implement					

Sales Forecast Model Template

Salesperson _____

Account	Proposed Product	Become Aware (0%)	Gain Initial Info (25%)	Gain In-Depth (50%)	Justify Internally (75%)	Buy (100%)	Revenue Opportunity	Factored Forecast $
Total							$	$

Measure Your Progress and Make Adjustments—Reporting Template Checklist
(at least monthly)

- Have you collected all of the necessary data on sales messages? on marketing activities and costs?
- Do you need to adjust the collection method to collect data more effectively or efficiently?
- Are you reporting results frequently enough to allow team members to make adjustments in their areas of responsibility?
- What results were achieved?
- Is there any other information needed to evaluate your progress? If yes, how will you get it?
- Is your progress behind, on, or ahead of the quantity and elapsed time targets?
- How can you improve?
- Do you need to reevaluate your target quantities? customer actions and stage in the Buying Cycle? business goals?
- Should you reduce, sustain, reallocate or increase your investment in this customer's Buying Cycle?
- Have you shared your finding with your own team? with others in the company as appropriate?

Manage Yourself and Others from an ROI Perspective

Part of managing yourself and others from an ROI perspective is the agreement between the employee and the employer to have the employee held accountable for results. This implies several things:

- The agreement to create an ROI-based plan
- The agreement to track and measure that plan
- The agreement to report back the results
- The agreement to measure the employee on the above three items
- The agreement to reward the employee on the above three items (with bonuses for exemplary business results)

The bottom line here is you get what you measure. If you want people to focus on activities in a frenetic pace, then measure them that way and that's what you'll get. If you want people to manage themselves, their time and their money from an ROI and business perspective, then measure them that way and you will get the results you really want, namely, profit!

Job Plan Checklist

Everyone in your company, including you, should have a job plan, which should include:

- Your roles/responsibilities
- The business goals that you will attain or contribute to (this means revenue)
- The marketing results that you will attain or contribute to (this means movement of the customer through the Buying Cycle)
- The skills and knowledge that you will develop as a result of this job plan (over a specific period of time)
- What you need from Management to help you achieve your goals
- How often you agree to report against your plan

We would strongly suggest that you do monthly reports. That way it is easy to correct your course if what you are doing does not match with your Management's expectations.

KEY LEARNINGS CHECKLIST

☑ Your people will do what you measure them to do. If you measure activities, that's what you'll get: more activities. If you measure movement through the customer Buying Cycle, that's what you'll get: more of a business focus, more revenue and more results.

☑ You should focus yourself and your people on:

- Business Results = Revenue/Profit
- Marketing and Sales Results = Movement of the Customer through the Buying Cycle

☑ If you want results from an ROI perspective, then you must measure yourself and others on the results achieved. This means:

- Create an ROI-based plan
- Empower a team of people not only to create the plan but to go out and implement it
- Track and measure the plan
- Report back the results
- Measure the employee on the results
- Reward the employee on the results

☑ Everyone in the company, including you, should have a job plan.

13

An Example of a
Complete Plan

Whe have provided an example of a complete business plan in this chapter. Please note that all of the examples used in *The Buck Starts Here* are based on real business situations that we have encountered. In most cases, we have changed company names, product types, hit ratios, and other factors to guarantee the confidentiality of our clients. These examples are intended to be a template for you to use to create your own integrated Sales and Marketing plans quickly and easily. Please note that the activities chosen by companies for the best ROI are italicized in the Sales and Marketing Mix Analysis charts.

CompuSys Company Example: Business Goal Segmentation

CompuSys Company is an imaginary international company that manufactures computers—mostly high-end ($500K and up) and mid-range ($175K–250K) computer systems. The firm specializes in fault-tolerant systems—systems that do not stop operating; they must run continuously. The company sells mostly to insurance companies, telecommunications companies and health care institutions that need a system that will not go down for their mission critical applications.

Their product set is as follows:

- High-end computers
- Mid-range computers
- Service (maintenance and repair)
- Technical consulting

This plan focuses on achieving the business plan for the Southwest District of the United States for making its numbers. The current fiscal year's revenue quota is projected at $7,750,000. Next year, CompuSys expects the Southwest to grow 10%. It also expects to sell more systems and services through resellers. The following is an example of CompuSys's Southwest District's Business Goal Segmentation.

Step 1—Determine Revenue Objectives: Southwest District

Current Fiscal Year	Fiscal Year +1	Fiscal Year +2
$7,750,000	$9,300,000	$11,160,000

Step 2—Determine Target Products or Geographies or Industries or Channels of Distribution That Will Drive Your Revenue

Since the Southwest *is* a geography, CompuSys has chosen not to break down its revenue by cities or counties within the Southwest. Although geography is not important to the Southwest, the channels of distribution within the products being sold certainly are. Therefore, the Southwest's first cut is of CompuSys products:

CURRENT YEAR

Product	% of Revenue Expected	$ Expected
Mid range	83%	$6.45M
High end	13%	$1.00M
Repair service	4%	$0.30M
Technical consulting	—	—
Total	100%	$7.75M

As you can see, CompuSys's mid-range products are driving the bulk of Southwest District's revenue.

Step 3—Identify the Channels of Distribution within the Products or Services That Will Achieve Your Revenue Objectives

CURRENT YEAR
PRODUCT MID-RANGE SYSTEMS =$6,450 Million

Channel of Distribution	New Accounts	Installed Accounts	Total Revenue
Direct sales force	$2.36M 80%	$2.1M 60%	$4.46M 69%
Resellers	$590K 20%	$1.4M 40%	$1.99M 31%
Total	$2.95M 100%	$3.5M 100%	$6.45M 100%

Step 4—Identify the Components That Will Achieve Your Revenue Objectives

PRODUCT: MID-RANGE SYSTEMS
CURRENT YEAR

Channel of Distribution	New Business	Installed Accounts	Total Revenue
Direct sales force	$2.36M 80% Avg. Sale Price = $175K # of Sales Needed = 14	$2.1M 60% Avg. Sale Price = $250K #of Sales Needed = 9	$4.46M 69%
Resellers	$590K 20% Avg. Sale Price = $150K # of Sales Needed = 4	$1.4M 40% Avg. Sale Price = $200K # of Sales Needed = 7	$1.99M 31%
Total	$2.95M 100%	$3.5M 100%	$6.45M 100%

Developing Successful Sales and Marketing Strategies: CompuSys Company

Describe Your Business Objectives

- Sales and marketing strategy for:
  Mid-Range Systems. We plan to drive $6.45M in Mid-Range Systems in the Southwest this fiscal year. We will focus this plan on selling $2.36M to new accounts through our sales force.

- Product:
  The average sale price of a Mid-Range System is $175K through our internal sales force.

  Total Revenue for this Plan: $2.36M
  For the Period Beginning 1/96, Ending 12/96

Describe Your Prospects

- Identify whom you will be selling to, by title:

	TITLE
Decision maker	CIO; VP, Engineering
Financial approver	CFO
Influencer	Key technical people within the corporation:
	Systems integrator
	Network manager
	Systems manager
Technical evaluator	Same as Influencer
Recommender	Same as Technical evaluator
Approver	Same as Decision maker

- **Describe the factors that will help you qualify prospects** (consider revenue, number of employees, profits, number of locations, budget, etc.): *Companies with greater than 50K transactions per day.*

- **Describe where the prospects are located** (territory, city, state/province, country, worldwide): *Southwest, U.S.*

- **Describe which industries or segments are the best prospects, or describe other factors that might influence your strategy** (consider industries, your installed base, a competitive installed base, etc.): *Due to the thrust of this product, we will focus on selling to new accounts. Industries to be focused on include:*

  — Distribution
  — Insurance
  — Telecommunications
  — Health care
  — Financial services
  — Government

Based on the above, who is *most* critical to your success?

Title: Key Technical Recommender (systems integrator, network manager, systems manager) We have chosen the Key Technical Recommender to focus on because their recommendation (in this particular market) is the equivalent of a buy decision. The CIO, who is technically the decision maker, almost always defers to the recommendation of this group.

List the secondary target(s) of your sales and marketing strategy:
Title: VP of Engineering
Title: CIO

CompuSys Company Example—Identifying the Customer's Buying Cycle

MID-RANGE SYSTEMS

Describe your short-term and long-term goals for these prospects:

Short-term goals

Recommend a Mid-Range System to CIO.

Long-term goals

Be a reference.

Describe the major checkpoints or buying actions the typical prospect will take to move through the Buying Cycle:

Actions

Describe needs

Learn about products

Inquire about CompuSys solution

Ask for product literature

Define the buying process

Evaluate CompuSys

Coordinate the two companies' efforts

Customer Buying Cycle Worksheet

For **Technical Evaluator**

Total Revenue **$2.36M**

Period Beginning **1/96**

Period Ending **12/96**

20 Recommen-dations

Qty		Weeks
20	Recommend: **Recommend CompuSys to CIO.**	2
50	Evaluate our solution: **Evaluate our solution. Financially justify system.**	4-8
100	Involvement: **Work with us to define specific needs & solutions.**	2-4
300	Basic fact finding: **Dialog with us about their needs/our solutions.** Share needs with us.	2-4
500	Awareness: **Share needs with us.**	1

1,000 Key Influencers

Total Time = 11–19 weeks
(2¾ mos–4¾ mos)

Note: We are assuming that 20 recommendations will give us 14 buys.

CompuSys Company—Sales and Marketing Operations Plan

BUY/SELL CYCLE   Stage __Awareness__

Target audience title:
___Key Influencer___

Number of people in audience:
___1,000___
(How many are you starting with at this point?)

Action you want the audience to take to move forward in the Buying Cycle:
___Become aware of the need for CompuSys Mid-Range Systems___

Number of people needed to take this action:
___500___

Sales Messages

- CompuSys's "continuous uptime" will allow you to have a system that is up and running constantly. This ensures that your mission-critical applications will never go down.
- Going down for even a minute can cost you a fortune (and in the case of hospitals can mean the loss of lives). CompuSys's Mid-Range Systems guarantee you constant system availability at a reasonable cost.

Technical Evaluator's Business Environment	Technical Evaluator's Business and Personal Needs	Features/ Characteristics of Our Mid-Range Systems	Our Competitive Advantage	Impact on Customer's Business
Control costs Shrinking margins Keeping good people	Ensure the systems operate at 100% at all times.	Highly reliable	Most reliable product on market, with a 99.9% uptime *Proof:* Article written by *Computer Times* magazine	Save you money in system downtime. *Proof:* BNA Company testimonial (continuous uptime has saved them millions in lost production and lost sales)
	Control technical costs.	Extremely cost-effective	Due to our high uptime, dollar for dollar, our Mid-Range Systems have the lowest per unit price (10–20% more effective than our competition). *Proof:* same article	Save you money compared with our competition. *Proof:* independent study done by a well-known research firm
	Get the backlog of technical changes done to specification.			

Sales and Marketing Mix Analysis
for the Awareness Stage of the Buying Cycle

Sales and Marketing Activity (trade shows, seminars, etc.)	Quantity Required (No. of people)	No. of People Who Will Act (projected) (C)	Material Prep and Delivery Costs (D)	Total Sales Costs (E)	Total Costs (columns D + E) = (F)	ROI (column F ÷ column C)
Phone calls by sales reps	500	300		1,000 calls @ 5 min/call = 5,000 min = 83.3 hrs = 3⅓ hrs/sales rep for 25 sales reps	83.3 hrs of sales time @ $500/hr = $41,650	$138.83
Direct mail	500	100	$3,000		$3,000	$ 30.00
Phone calls by sales reps and direct mail*	500	500	$3,000	1,000 calls @ 5 min/call = 5,000 min = 83.3 hrs = 3⅓ hrs/sales rep for 25 sales reps	83.3 hrs of sales time @ $500/hr = $41,650 plus $3,000 (material cost) = $44,650	$ 89.30
Seminars (direct mail invites the customer)	500	Not applicable for this stage of buying cycle	N/A			
Surveys/questionnaires	500	10	$5,000		$5,000	$500.00
Ads	500	10	$7,500		$7,500	$750.00
Roundtable seminar	500	Not applicable for this stage of buying cycle	N/A		$11,500	$230.00

*CompuSys decided it could not do direct mail alone and get the results it wanted even though the investment per result was the best. The firm needed to incorporate phone calls by the sales reps with direct mail in order to achieve the wanted results.

Select the Sales and Marketing Mix for the Awareness Stage of the Buying Cycle

Choose the sales and marketing mix that you believe will be successful. Experiment with new techniques. Determine, in advance, how you will track what is working and what isn't working.

Sales and Marketing Mix	Quantity of Results Required	What Needs to Be Tracked	How	What This Will Tell Me
Phone calls by sales reps	500	– # Phoned – When – # Responses 1. Interest level 2. Budget 3. Internal project definition 4. Time frame 5. If they use integrators	Log kept by Sales	• Right quantity? • Success rate • Bad addresses • Interest now and in the future • Like/dislike/ preferences
Direct mail	500	# Responses • By business reply card • By phone • By fax	Log kept by Marketing	• Right quantity? • Success rate • Bad addresses • Interest now and in the future • Like/dislike/ preferences

Carry Out the Effort for the Awareness Stage of the Buying Cycle

Actions That Need to Be Taken	How Long It Will Take	When Due	By Whom
Buy list for phone calls by sales reps/direct mail	2–3 weeks	1/15	Marketing—Cindy
Create mail piece	4–6 weeks	2/1	Jim
Create phone call script	2 weeks	2/1	Cindy
Design daily log/tracking sheets	1 week	2/1	Cindy
Send mail piece to production house		2/15	Jim
Start phone calls		Week of 3/1	Sales reps

Sales and Marketing Mix Analysis
for the Basic Fact-Finding Stage of the Buying Cycle

Sales and Marketing Activity (trade shows, seminars, etc.)	Quantity Required (No. of people)	No. of People Who Will Act (projected) (C)	Material Prep and Delivery Costs (D)	Total Sales Costs (E)	Total Costs (columns D + E) = (F)	ROI (column F ÷ column C)
Seminars (direct mail invitations to the customer)	300	150	10 seminars @ $500 ea = $5,000		$5,000	$ 33.33
Sales calls currently without checklist of objectives	300	100		150 sales calls @ 3.0 hrs/call = 450 hrs @ $500/hr = $225K	$225K	$2,250.00
Sales calls with checklist of objectives	300	100		100 sales calls @ 2.5 hrs/call = 250 hrs @ $500/hr = $125K	$125K	$1,250.00
Seminars, then sales calls by the sales reps after the seminar*	300	300	10 seminars @ $500 ea = $5,000	300 sales calls @ 2.0 hrs/call = 600 hrs @ $500/hr = $300K	$300K + $5K = $305K	$1,016.67
Roundtable seminar at a trade show	300	10	$20K		$20,000	$2,000.00
Trade shows	300	5	$20K		$20,000	$4,000.00

*CompuSys decided that if it changed the direct mail and phone call scripts/pieces in the awareness stage, it could bump up attendance at the seminars. The firm also decided that seminars by themselves would not achieve the needed results. But seminars could definitely give quite a few customers some basic information that would cut down on the time needed for the sales rep to make a face-to-face call. So, based on this analysis the seminars followed by sales rep calls were chosen as the best activity with the best ROI.

CompuSys decided that by implementing a standard sales call (with objectives clearly stated for each sales rep), it could significantly cut down on the number of sales calls needed at this stage. Currently, it needed two or three sales calls, with two or three people on each call. With the standard sales call checklist and proper training of the sales reps, it could bring this down to one sales call per customer at this stage of the buying cycle.

Select the Sales and Marketing Mix for the Basic Fact-Finding Stage of the Buying Cycle

Choose the sales and marketing mix that you believe will be successful. Experiment with new techniques. Determine, in advance, how you will track what is working and what isn't working.

Sales and Marketing Mix	Quantity of Results Required	What Needs to Be Tracked	How	What This Will Tell Me
Seminars	300 attendees @ 10 seminars	• # Invitations • # Attendees • # No-shows • Titles of attendees • Pre/post evaluation	Sign-in sheets logged by secretary	• Quantity invited • Success rate • No-show rate • Right people came • Like/dislike/ preferences
Sales calls by sales reps *after* the seminars	300 sales calls	Basic fact-finding check-list: 1. Customer is willing to hear proposal. 2. Customer is willing to set up meeting with the CIO. 3. Reaction of customer to potential savings	Log kept by sales reps	• # Customers moving through Buying Cycle • Their reaction to our sales messages

Carry Out the Effort for the Basic Fact-Finding Stage of the Buying Cycle

Actions That Need to Be Taken	How Long It Will Take	When Due	By Whom
Book conference room for seminars	1 week	1/15	Cindy
Book internal speakers	2 weeks	1/15	Cindy
Book customer guest speakers	2 weeks	1/15	Cindy
Train sales on standard checklist call	3 weeks	1/15	Mike
Make sure demo is up and running for seminar		2/1	Chuck

Sales and Marketing Mix Analysis for the Involvement (In-Depth-Information) Stage of the Buying Cycle

Sales and Marketing Activity (trade shows, seminars, etc.)	Quantity Required (No. of people)	No. of People Who Will Act (projected) (C)	Material Prep and Delivery Costs (D)	Total Sales Costs (E)	Total Costs (columns D + E) = (F)	ROI (column F + column C)
One or two face-to-face calls by sales reps plus tech specialist	100	100		Total of 400 sales calls @ 2–3 hrs ea = $400–600K	$400–600K	
One face-to-face sales call by sales reps with regional manager to the CIO	100	100		125 (or so) sales calls with CIOs @ 1.5 hrs ea = $93,750	$93,750	
Boilerplate created by Marketing: • Quality proposal • Quality analysis • Quality ROI model	100	100	3–4 man weeks = $6,250 + $2,000 in production costs		$ 8,250	
Total of the above three			$8,250	$493,750–693,750	$502K–702K	$5,020–$7,020

*CompuSys decided to do all three of the above activities. They also decided that by putting very specific sales call objectives/checklists in place, giving proper training and producing excellent-quality marketing materials/boilerplate, it could cut its current number of sales calls at this stage as follows:

TODAY

- 5 or 6 face-to-face sales calls between CompuSys sales rep/tech specialist and key influencer customer
- Reference (customer) visit to corporate
- 2–5 man-days spent on a proposal

PROPOSED

- 3 or 4 face-to-face sales calls
- Move these visits to the next stage of the customer Buying Cycle, where the customer is more committed to the CompuSys solution.
- 1 man/day spent on a proposal (using high-quality boilerplate described above

Select the Sales and Marketing Mix for the Involvement (In-Depth-Information) Stage of the Buying Cycle

Choose the sales and marketing mix that you believe will be successful. Experiment with new techniques. Determine, in advance, how you will track what is working and what isn't working.

Sales and Marketing Mix	Quantity of Results Required	What Needs to Be Tracked	How	What This Will Tell Me
Face-to-face sales calls by sales rep and tech specialist	100 sales calls	Involvement (in-depth-information) checklist: 1. Key influencer is willing to set up meeting between CompuSys regional manager and CIO: "No CIO, No Go." 2. Resource commitment from customer	Log kept by sales reps	• # Customers moving through Buying Cycle • Their reaction to our sales messages

Carry Out the Effort for the Involvement (In-Depth-Information) Stage of the Buying Cycle

Actions That Need to Be Taken	How Long It Will Take	When Due	By Whom
Create boilerplate: • Proposal • Analysis • ROI models	4–6 weeks	2/15	Tom
Two or three selected sales reps + one regional manager review Tom's boilerplate every week (or as needed).	Same		John Phil Ray Bill
Book customer guest speakers	2 weeks	1/15	Cindy
Train sales on in-depth product information needed by customer at involvement stage, plus train sales on boilerplate created.		3/1	Mike Tom

Sales and Marketing Mix Analysis for the Evaluation Stage of the Buying Cycle

Sales and Marketing Activity (trade shows, seminars, etc.)	Quantity Required (No. of people)	No. of People Who Will Act (projected) (C)	Material Prep and Delivery Costs (D)	Total Sales Costs (E)	Total Costs (columns D + E) = (F)	ROI (column F ÷ column C)
Demos	50	30			30 demos @ 3 hrs ea with 2 CompuSys people @ $500/hr = $90K	$3,000
Reference phone calls made from prospect to installed customer	50	60			0	0
Customer visits	50	10			10 customer visits @ $4,000 ea (includes all people time and materials) = $40,000	$4,000
Seed unit	50	5			$10,000 (for each seed unit) ✕ 5 = $50,000 (includes all costs)	$10,000
Total cost of above						$3,000–10,000

Note: CompuSys decided to do all of the above activities. They also decided it would not give out seed units unless: (1) It was absolutely necessary to close the sale, (2) the dollar volume of the sale was greater than $300K. CompuSys also decided to rename seed units within the company to Phase I implementation, thereby implying a change in attitude. The firm was not providing demo units to try out; it was letting a customer install early and was charging the customer for this service.

CompuSys also decided that all four of the above activities would be needed to achieve the results it wanted. It felt that the customers who saw the demos in the field probably would not want to attend a corporate customer visit.

Select the Sales and Marketing Mix for the Evaluation Stage of the Buying Cycle

Choose the sales and marketing mix that you believe will be successful. Experiment with new techniques. Determine, in advance, how you will track what is working and what isn't working.

Sales and Marketing Mix	Quantity of Results Required	What Needs to Be Tracked	How	What This Will Tell Me
Demos made by sales rep and tech specialist	30 demos	Evaluation checklist: 1. CIO presentation is scheduled. 2. Trial close is made by sales rep. 3. Contract is signed by CIO.	Log kept by sales reps	• # Customers moving through Buying Cycle • Their reaction to our sales messages

Carry Out the Effort for the Evaluation Stage of the Buying Cycle

Actions That Need to Be Taken	How Long It Will Take	When Due	By Whom
Create a phase I installation checklist and customer expectation/agreement package.	2–3 weeks	3/15	Bill
Create a customer visit experience. Schedule/select the CompuSys execs needed to close the sale.	2 weeks	3/15	Cindy

Sales and Marketing Mix Analysis
for the Recommend-to-CIO Stage of the Buying Cycle

Sales and Marketing Activity (trade shows, seminars, etc.)	Quantity Required (No. of people)	No. of People Who Will Act (projected) (C)	Material Prep and Delivery Costs (D)	Total Sales Costs (E)	Total Costs (columns D + E) = (F)	ROI (column F ÷ column C)
Face-to-face presentation (CompuSys sales team plus customer team with CIO)	20	20		20 presentations @ 3–4 people per presentation × 6 hrs (development plus delivery) = $180K–240K	$180K–240K	$9,000–12,000

Select the Sales and Marketing Mix for the Recommend-to-CIO Stage of the Buying Cycle

Choose the sales and marketing mix that you believe will be successful. Experiment with new techniques. Determine, in advance, how you will track what is working and what isn't working.

Sales and Marketing Mix	Quantity of Results Required	What Needs to Be Tracked	How	What This Will Tell Me
Presentation to CIO	20	Recommend checklist: 1. CIO presentation is completed. 2. CIO buys off on final implementation plan.	Log kept by sales reps	• # Customers moving through Buying Cycle • Their reaction to our sales messages

CompuSys's Key Influencer Buy Cycle

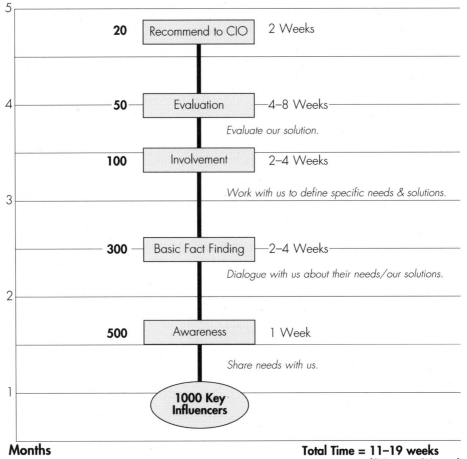

Months

TRB Consulting Group, Inc. ©1994

Total Time = 11–19 weeks
(2¾ mos–4¾ mos)

CompuSys's Key Influencer Buy Cycle

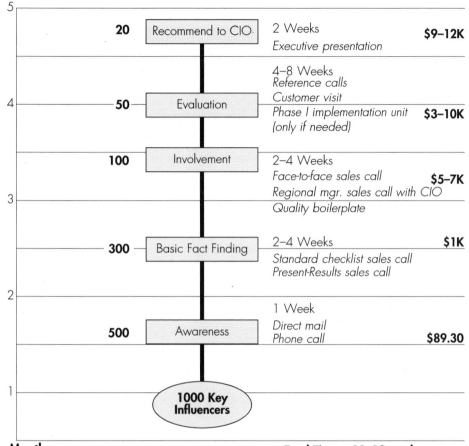

20	Recommend to CIO	2 Weeks *Executive presentation*	$9–12K
50	Evaluation	4–8 Weeks *Reference calls* *Customer visit* *Phase I implementation unit* *(only if needed)*	$3–10K
100	Involvement	2–4 Weeks *Face-to-face sales call* *Regional mgr. sales call with CIO* *Quality boilerplate*	$5–7K
300	Basic Fact Finding	2–4 Weeks *Standard checklist sales call* *Present-Results sales call*	$1K
500	Awareness	1 Week *Direct mail* *Phone call*	$89.30

1000 Key Influencers

Months

TRB Consulting Group, Inc. ©1994

Total Time = 11–19 weeks
(2¾ mos–4¾ mos)

Total Sales and Marketing
Investment per Recommendation =
$18,100–30,100

Epilogue:
Where Are Sales and Marketing
Going in the Future?

*U*p to this point in the book, we have focused on what is wrong with Sales and Marketing and we have provided a simple methodology and tools to help you create more powerful and profitable sales and marketing programs.

Before we proceed to talk about the future, let's put some things into perspective.

First, in the thirty-plus years we have been in Sales, Marketing and Management, we have never heard of sales quotas going down! They always go up. After a hard-fought, successful year, the sales reps and managers face 20%, 30%, 50%, 100% increases in quota, and they valiantly try to achieve them. When they miss these new objectives, we frequently tell them that they have failed, even though they may have produced 50% or 70% more than the prior year—*without* 50% more resources, and certainly, without 50% (or any) more compensation. "It's Sales' fault." Baloney!

Second, Sales and Marketing are achieving these dramatic gains without having the state-of-the-art tools to improve their efficiency. They are frequently working with inadequate and obsolete systems and spend more time on internal administrivia and inefficiency than on customer contact.

Third, Management is frequently the obstacle to sales and marketing progress. One of the questions that we ask at the conclusion of our seminars is, "What else do you need?" The most frequent response, is "Management buy-in." If Management continues to motivate people to do more activities (more sales calls, more trade shows, more lead generation) instead of higher-quality, results-oriented activities, that is what it will get: a lot more untargeted, unfocused activities.

In summary, we believe that today's Sales and Marketing organizations are doing an admirable job. Like the best athletes, each and every year they set new goals and achieve their personal best. It's time that we recognized them for their achievements and realized how important their contribution is to a company's success.

With that in mind, what do we see changing in the coming years? How will the best Sales and Marketing companies develop even leaner, more efficient sales and marketing machines that are flexible enough to adapt to the needs of the future? How will they organize? How will they train people? What tools will they provide? Here are some thoughts and observations on some of the changes we expect to see in Sales and Marketing.

MANAGEMENT WILL TREAT SALES AND MARKETING LIKE A BUSINESS

Sales and Marketing shouldn't be perceived as "black magic." They consist of a set of processes that should have a purpose in mind: to generate business (revenue).

If you need to increase manufacturing capacity by 50%, do you simply tell the VP of Manufacturing, "Just do it"? Of course not. A plan is put in place to ensure that the right capacity is available, that quality can get measured, that costs can be controlled, etc. Rarely is that type of planning and management focus given to Sales and Marketing.

Sales and marketing expense is buried under SG&A (Sales, General and Administrative) in financial reports.

Hundreds of thousands and millions of dollars are spent on campaigns without definable, explainable, measurable business objectives.

We threaten and cajole Sales and Marketing management into attaining impossible or bad business goals under the stated or implied threat that "if you don't make the number, we'll find someone who will." Stop! We have to change, and Sales and Marketing management can't do it all. The management team must change the way Sales and Marketing is viewed and treated. Sales and Marketing is not just a service organization to your company. A good, integrated Sales and Marketing organization is critical to product development, efficient manufacturing and distribution, and good financial controls—critical to every element of a business.

The management team, therefore, should expect and demand that Sales and Marketing be managed with the same disciplines that are expected from Manufacturing, Engineering, Finance, and other critical areas of the business. The processes involved in building a sale should be as well-defined as the processes in manufacturing a product. What *are* the processes? How much does each step cost? Where are the likely points of failure? How can we ensure quality? How do we monitor and evaluate the processes so we can continually refine and improve the process?

We can't hide behind canned excuses any more: "Every sale is different." "We don't have the systems in place." "It will cost more to track." The same phony excuses were heard from Finance and Manufacturing twenty years ago.

The basic business issue is, "Can this product be sold and marketed profitably?" Few companies can answer that question accurately, based on facts. Companies that know how much it costs to manufacture a product do not know how much it costs to sell it. They may know gross profit by product, but they do not know which products are profitable and which lose money—after the cost of sales and marketing.

The companies that realize the importance of Sales and Marketing and put the processes in place to manage Sales and Marketing as efficiently as Manufacturing will be in a position to optimize their profit in the increasingly competitive marketplace. They will know where the costs are, where the inefficiencies are and where to tweak, change or reengineer for maximum efficiency. They will know how to create the efficient and profitable sales and marketing processes that make it easy for their customers to buy from them.

ALL LEVELS OF SALES AND MARKETING MANAGEMENT MUST START ASKING THE TOUGH QUESTIONS:

- "What results can we expect from that investment in marketing or sales?"
- "Who is the target customer, and what actions will the customer take as a result of this activity/program?"
- "How does that investment compare with other alternatives that we've evaluated?"
- "Specifically, how does that activity or program contribute to our business/revenue objectives?"
- "How will we track results so we know whether the activity or program is working?"
- "What will we learn so that we can improve?"

The change from black magic to business management must begin at the senior management level. Senior management must stop authorizing the expenditures of vast sums on sales and marketing programs that can't be explained or that do not have clearly defined business objectives.

If you or your people can't answer these types of questions, don't fund the project until you get good answers. If the program doesn't make sense to you, it probably won't make sense to your customers either.

The bottom line to Sales and Marketing should be, "What's the business case?" Are these sales and marketing expenditures spending money or investing money? Will they just increase sales and grow the business, or will they do it profitably? Is it a good business decision or not?

LEADERS WILL TRAIN SALESPEOPLE TO BE BUSINESSPEOPLE

Teaching sales skills is not enough. The most productive salespeople in the future will have a good combination of sales *and* business skills. They will have the skills and knowledge to run their territories like a business, understanding how to leverage their limited resources for optimum results.

Among the types of skills that need to be taught are:

- How to set goals—both business and personal
- How to segment and prioritize business opportunities: How good are they? How do they contribute to the business/personal goals mentioned above?
- How to plan: How to develop and execute plans to achieve the stated goals
- How to monitor and measure plans to learn how and what to improve
- How to leverage various marketing techniques (direct mail, telemarketing, etc.) to optimize productivity

Depending on the selling environment, some salespeople should become thoroughly familiar with and able to understand financial statements to improve business relationships with customers and business partners. At a minimum, they need to understand that every sales call they make costs money; every brochure, seminar, trade show and telephone call costs money; and every discount they give impacts the bottom line. They need to understand that making sales quota is not enough. They need to do it profitably.

Salespeople who master these skills will be your sales managers, product managers and marketing managers of the future. The time to teach these skills is now, so that they are ingrained when salespeople assume greater responsibility.

You don't have to wait that long to realize benefits from salespeople with these skills, however. Not only will they start selling better, more profitable business quicker, but they also will be excellent resources for understanding and dissecting your selling process. Lock a few good salespeople in a room with a good facilitator and challenge them to develop a more efficient sales process, and you will be pleasantly surprised by the results. For best results, put a few customers in the room too!

IT'S LONG OVERDUE: INFORMATION TECHNOLOGY WILL BE APPLIED TO SALES AND MARKETING

Let's face it. The application of information technology (IT) to the sales and marketing process is twenty years behind the times. Every other part of business is on the third, fourth or fifth generation (or more) of technology, and sales is just starting to get laptops with "productivity tools." Sure, you get sales reports and quota reports, but how current are they? Are they really decision support tools? Do they help manage the business more effectively, or do they just state what happened last month?

Companies that can tell how many minutes and seconds it took to build a part don't have the slightest idea how many man-hours, days or weeks it takes to close a sale.

Companies that have databases of every part and engineering change that ever existed don't have a database that salespeople can use to send a mailing to customers of product X in their territory.

Coming up with "quick and dirty" fixes will not solve the problem and may, in fact, create more problems.

What is needed is an Integrated Sales and Marketing Management System equivalent to the most advanced manufacturing, engineering and financial systems that exist today.

The Integrated Sales and Marketing Management System must look at the total process of sales and marketing, not just sales tracking or lead generation. The system must contain prospect, market and customer databases, sales histories, sales projections, forecasting tools, planning tools, management tools and more. It must be designed around the total *system* of sales and marketing, not just the most obvious or biggest problems.

Without powerful IT systems, Sales and Marketing cannot make the great strides in efficiency, quality, cost control and customer satisfaction that we have seen in Manufacturing. While some companies are using IT effectively and even changing the way they sell product to customers because of IT, we have not seen the great leap forward. But the payback from such a system is enormous:

- Increased sales productivity
- Reduced cost of sales and marketing
- Increased customer satisfaction
- Elimination of unnecessary marketing and advertising expenditures

What amazes us is that these systems are not yet available. Sales and Marketing (buried in Sales, General and Administrative) remains the largest unmanaged expense on the corporate financial statements—the black hole of the balance sheet. How long can it stay that way?

SALES AND MARKETING WILL BE INTEGRATED

More companies will move toward selling teams to develop, implement and manage the sales and marketing of products.

The selling teams will be cross-functional, or cross-skilled, including appropriate representation from Sales, Marketing, Communications, Engineering, Product Development, Product Management, Finance, etc. Together, they will develop and evaluate the total business case from product development to announcement through to product replacement.

We like to think of this team as a group of entrepreneurs putting together a business plan to get funding for their business venture—for the product(s) and markets that they are responsible for. The team's goal is to develop the business case strong enough to get the venture capitalists (the company) to fund the project and then to manage the business as a *real* business.

The team will get involved in the very early stages of product development, before major funding commitments are made. The team's mission is to ensure that the products being developed can be brought to market and sold—successfully, efficiently and profitably.

Using the approach outlined in this book, the team can easily identify what they know and don't know about each business issue, be it revenue objectives, competition, target customer audience Buying Cycles or product requirements. The team will be able to quickly identify the obstacles standing in the way of their mutual success, and will develop plans to overcome those obstacles. If the team determines that a product cannot be brought to market and sold efficiently and profitably, then that product should not be funded until the obstacles are removed.

The members of the team may change over time, and the team's focus may shift as the product moves from conception to customer, but it is best if the team stays together as if it really were a "company." The swinging-door approach to product management (where people come and go frequently) leads to product failures with absolutely no accountability and, more important, no continuity to help prevent repeating the same mistakes.

The team approach has worked in Engineering, Manufacturing and other business areas. It will work in Sales and Marketing as well.

FINANCE'S ROLE IN SALES AND MARKETING WILL CHANGE

In the past, Finance's role in the *business* of Sales and Marketing has been limited. When margins get squeezed, Finance wants to reduce sales and marketing budgets and watch the expense accounts more closely. When sales are great, Finance opens the purse a little wider and allocates bigger budgets and more spending. When salespeople are very successful and start earning large commissions, Finance wants to cap their earnings because they're "making too much."

More often than not, that type of knee-jerk reaction results in poor business decisions. To make better business decisions, Finance needs to play a more active role in Sales and Marketing—the role of educators, planners and team players.

As an educator, Finance needs to teach Sales and Marketing about the business case—the profit and loss of sales and marketing. What products have strong gross margins, and why, should be part of the education process for all concerned. The effect of discounts on the bottom line should be another point in the education of Sales and Marketing. The list continues: the importance of good sales forecasts and the cost of bad forecasts; the impact of a poor marketing campaign on profitability, etc.

The important thing is that financial expertise and knowledge must be taken out of the closet and shared with Sales and Marketing. Finance and Sales and Marketing must become true business partners.

Armed with this knowledge, Sales and Marketing will make better business decisions and create better compensation plans and profitable sales and marketing programs. More competitive and focused sales and marketing compensation plans will hold in check the cost of sales attrition and new-hire-training ramp uptime and expense—all of which impact the bottom line.

As a planner, Finance needs to get more involved in Sales and Marketing. Finance needs to understand the sales and marketing processes of the company as well as Sales and Marketing understands them. Finance can help Sales and Marketing in many ways. It can help:

- Develop the best pricing strategies.
- Identify the true costs of closing a sale.
- Develop the investment strategy for sales and marketing.
- Develop the business case on the profit and loss of various products and markets.
- Evaluate different marketing techniques to find the most efficient.
- Negotiate contracts with vendors.

These are simply a few of the value-added services that Finance can contribute to the integrated Sales and Marketing team.

The contribution that Finance can make to the Sales and Marketing management team can be enormous. Since most sales and marketing people do not have strong financial backgrounds, Finance can provide the discipline and skills necessary to develop strong, profit-oriented sales and marketing strategies and the discipline and controls to implement, manage, evaluate and improve those strategies over time.

CHANNELS OF DISTRIBUTION WILL CONTINUE TO EVOLVE

Companies use various channels to get product to their customers. In some cases that channel might be a company sales force that sells direct to the end customer. In other cases, the sale might be made through a direct mail, telemarketing or other program. In other cases, a company might employ multitiered distributors, wholesalers, dealers and retailers to get the product to market.

In many cases in the past, companies used various channels to increase their penetration, market share and revenue. Unfortunately, some of these "channels" have turned out to be inefficient, costly and damaging to a company's image and downright bad business.

In the future, companies will be more selective about the channels they choose. They will realize that focusing on just growing the business is not a good strategy; they must focus on profit. Some very well-known companies that focused on growth more than profit learned the hard way, as phenomenal growth resulted in some phenomenal losses.

Channels of distribution will be evaluated carefully to determine which are efficient, which are profitable and which truly add value, because *all* add cost.

Companies will ask the question, "If a channel can sell my product profitably, why can't *we* sell it profitably?"

After evaluating the *cost* of channel versus the *value add* provided by the channel, some companies will reduce or eliminate channels and do more direct sales; others will flatten the distribution process by eliminating some tiers; still others will work with the channel partner to increase the efficiency of the channel while reducing costs.

More people need to realize that the discount off list price that we give to our channel partners is really a payment to them to sell our product to their customers. These discounts vary widely, from 10% to 30% to 50% and sometimes more.

Instead of calling it a discount, incentive, margin, points or whatever else we call it, why don't we call it a *cost of sales and marketing*, because that is what it really is.

Changes to the distribution channel will occur not only because companies are demanding more value add and less cost. Change will be accelerated because of the way people want to *buy* products, from food to clothing to movies to computers. People will pay more for value and service where value and service are clearly defined and necessary. They will not pay for overhead *disguised* as value and service.

Channels will appear and disappear more quickly (look at the personal computer business, for example), and both producers and buyers of products may find that the channels that are moving products to the end user don't always work and can be downright frustrating.

More and more companies will find that excellent management of channels will provide pricing advantages and a competitive edge; companies with poor channel management will be left in the dust.

MORE COMPANIES WILL REALIZE THAT SALES AND MARKETING AND CUSTOMER SUPPORT HAVE VALUE

Not too long ago, the Vice President of Sales at a company in a very competitive market was explaining how his company sold premium products and charged as much as 30% more than their competitors. The products the company sold were luncheon meats—salami, bologna and the like.

We commented to him that some of our clients consider their products to be commodity products—products that cost thousands of dollars, not $4 a pound! He replied, "If *any* of my salespeople calls our products commodities, I'll fire him/her."

Think about it. Some people consider, for example, that personal computers are commodity products and that the only way to get a competitive advantage is by offering the lowest price.

Why then, when you walk through the breakfast cereal section of the grocery store, are some cereals priced at 20%, 30% and 40% more than similar cereals next to them on the shelf?

Products become "commodities" when companies run out of sales and marketing energy. They become commodities when these same companies quit the hard work of sales and marketing.

Before we proceed, let's take a quick look at a hypothetical company's financials on the next page.

Selling price (revenue)	$1,000
• Cost of goods sold (60% of selling price)	– 600
Gross profit	$ 400
• SG&A (Sales, General & Administrative) expense (30% of the selling price)	– 300
Profit (10%)	$ 100

If the $1,000 product above is being sold in a very competitive environment, and if Sales and Marketing consider it to be a "commodity" product, it is common to use discounting—"pricing actions"—to win the competitive battle. Since few people in Sales and Marketing look at the bottom line, it is common to see people discounting products like the one above by 10% or 15% or more.

In the above case, a 10% discount results in zero profit. A 15% discount results in a net loss.

Now, we are aware that some convoluted thinkers can justify such loss-leader sales tactics as due to the long-range impact of "some mumbo jumbo." We like to keep things simple. If somebody is going to continuously sell product at a loss, let it be your competitor, because if *you* sell product at a loss, you will eventually go out of business. Some people think that they will "make it up in volume." This kind of thinking is sheer nonsense.

Let's go a little further with our hypothetical product. When the competition gets hot and revenue goes down, what does Finance tend to do? Reduce expenses, of course. Cut back on those lunches and trips. Reduce the marketing budget. Increase quota. Cut commissions. Finance says things like, "We have to make these numbers *work*!"

Now, if the product is really *not* competitive and the only way that it can be sold is to sell it at a loss, then the company had better find another product or market or figure out how and where to sell it profitably, or get out of the business. If a company is selling products at a loss as a "holding action" until the next-generation product comes out, it must be extremely careful—it might be selling its next product at a loss, too!

Before a company quits, before it discounts itself out of business, before it calls its product a "commodity," look at another approach. Let's go back to our hypothetical company's financials. Remember, sales and marketing expense is buried in SG&A along with desks, pencils, electricity and water coolers. If we assume that half of SG&A is "G&A" and the other half is "sales and marketing," our financials look like this:

Selling price (revenue)	$1,000
• Cost of goods sold (60% of selling price)	– 600
Gross profit	$ 400
• SG&A (Sales, General & Administrative expense):	
G&A	– 150
Sales and Marketing	– 150
Profit (10%)	$ 100

Suppose that the company decides to *increase* its investment in sales and marketing instead of reducing sales and marketing expense. Suppose it decides to invest more money in finding more qualified leads, doing a better job of explaining the benefits of its products, increasing customer service, improving brand image and improving the quality of customer support? *Suppose that it decides to create competitive advantage not by discounting but by superior sales, marketing and customer support? What would happen?*

In the above example, a company can increase its sales spending in sales and marketing by more than 50% and still be better off in profit than by giving a 10% discount.

Surprised? Let's see, on page 216, how this works:

	With a 10% Discount	Increase Sales and Marketing by 50% (No Discount)
Selling price	$1,000	$1,000
• 10% discount	– 100	
Revenue	$ 900	$1,000
• Cost of goods sold (60% of selling price)	– 600	– 600
Gross profit	$ 300	$ 400
• SG&A (Sales, General & Administrative expense):		
G&A	– 150	– 150
Sales and Marketing	– 150	– 225*
Net Profit	$ 0	$ 25

*$225 on Sales and Marketing assumes 50% more than before; therefore an increase of $75.

Sure, this is a hypothetical case, but what are the numbers for *your* company? Are you in a similar situation? Are your salespeople prone to discount? Are you considering cutting back sales and marketing expenditures in order to control cost instead of using sales and marketing as a competitive weapon? Is cutting the marketing budget the correct business decision, or should you really be increasing the marketing budget?

The botttom line is that companies that integrate their Sales and Marketing team and bring good financial players on board will be looking at the total business case involved in these discussions and make better decisions.

NONE OF THIS WILL HAPPEN WITHOUT YOU

As we stated earlier, this is not rocket science. There is no magic or mystery to this business of sales and marketing. It is just common sense. It is just the practical application of business processes to Sales and

Marketing. True, there is a creative genius that makes sales and marketing work, too, but more of the so-called genius consists in hard work and knowing the basics.

We do not expect that you will necessarily agree with all we have discussed in this book, nor is it likely that you have all of the problems we described. If you agree with *any* of it and agree that Sales and Marketing has to change to increase efficiency and profitability, then that change must begin with you.

If you are in Sales, reevaluate what you are doing. Set your personal and business goals; segment and prioritize your business opportunities; develop a plan; strive to understand your customer's Buying Cycle and needs. Run your territory like a business. Improve the quality of your activities before increasing the quantity.

If you are in Marketing, don't allow yourself to get into activity mode, running from task to task, managing your to-do list and being caught in the Alice in Wonderland syndrome. Don't "spend the budget." *Invest* in marketing programs that are directly tied to business objectives. Measure the results of your programs so that you know what worked and what didn't work and why, so that you can have a process of continuing improvement. Don't work in a vacuum. Get Sales involved. Get customers involved. Get anyone and everyone involved who can contribute to your success. Spend your time and money as if *you* owned the business and were investing *your* money.

If you are in Engineering or Product Development, get those sales and marketing people involved now, not sixty days before the product is announced. Get Finance involved too. The communication problems among those four diverse cultures must be overcome. Developing a product and bringing it to market only to learn that it can't be sold profitably or doesn't meet customer needs is not fun and finger-pointing doesn't make it easier.

If you are in Finance, join the team. Become the educator; assist in planning. Complement the sales, marketing and engineering skills with your knowledge of financials and business processes.

If you are in Manufacturing, join the team. You bring valuable experience in the product creation, design *and* delivery to the customer. Remember that the integration of engineering and manufacturing processes also was not an easy transition. You have been there. You have a lot of knowledge to share.

If you are in IT, learn more about the total system of sales and marketing from product and market creation to obsolescence, because that's what a real sales and marketing system has to deal with.

If you are in the academic community, strive to balance the amount of theory with a good dose of practical sales and marketing knowledge. Too many students exit business and marketing schools with little or no practical knowledge about how to "do" sales and marketing. It takes years of experience for them to become somewhat rounded. It shouldn't take that long.

Senior executives have perhaps the most responsibility in effecting change. Your commitment is required to change your company from a *spend* focus to an *invest* focus. Your direction is required to tear down the walls between Sales, Marketing, Product Development and Finance so that effective selling teams can be created. You must ask, "What results do we expect from that investment in sales and marketing?" all the time, and you must stop funding programs that don't have clearly defined business goals. It is you who must insist that sales and marketing be managed as a business, and you who must insist that implementation of the implied changes becomes a reality. It is you who must demand accountability and measurement. Constantly challenge your staff to develop new and more profitable selling models that make it easier for your customers to buy—from you.

Whatever your role, whatever your position, continuously challenge the "way we've always done it in the past" mentality. Ask yourself, "Why are we doing this?" "What results should we expect?" "Is there a better way?" and "How will we monitor and measure this?" In due time, you will become a very proficient businessperson. Remember—it is up to you to begin the process of change. One person speaking his or her mind can affect the lives of many others. People will listen because what we've just talked about is common sense. It takes just one voice. Let it be yours.

Good Luck and Good Selling!

Appendix

This section contains all of the worksheets that were used in *The Buck Starts Here*. If you simply follow from one sheet to the other, you will have a finalized business plan. Remember, it is not necessary to overanalyze or go into analysis paralysis. Use the template as a thought process for good business decisions.

BUSINESS GOAL SEGMENTATION

Step 1—Determine Revenue Objectives

Current Fiscal Year	Fiscal Year +1	Fiscal Year +2

Step 2—Determine Target Geographies or Channels of Distribution

Note: Use whichever is the most important first cut of your data. If you are selling to only one geography and are using only one channel of distribution, go directly to step 3.

Geography	% of Revenue Expected	$ Expected
Total	100%	$

or

Channel of Distribution	% of Revenue Expected	$ Expected
Total	100%	$

Step 3—Identify the Products or Services That Will Achieve Your Revenue Objectives

If you used "Geography" in step 2, use this worksheet:

Product or Service	Geography _____	Geography _____	Geography _____	Total Revenue
	$ _____ _____ %	$ _____ _____ %	$ _____ _____ %	$ _____ _____ %
	$ _____ _____ %	$ _____ _____ %	$ _____ _____ %	$ _____ _____ %
	$ _____ _____ %	$ _____ _____ %	$ _____ _____ %	$ _____ _____ %
TOTAL	$ _____ _____ %	$ _____ _____ %	$ _____ _____ %	$ _____ 100%

If you used "Channel of Distribution" in step 2, use this worksheet:

Product or Service	Channel of Distribution _____	Channel of Distribution _____	Channel of Distribution _____	Total Revenue
	$ _____ _____ %	$ _____ _____ %	$ _____ _____ %	$ _____ _____ %
	$ _____ _____ %	$ _____ _____ %	$ _____ _____ %	$ _____ _____ %
	$ _____ _____ %	$ _____ _____ %	$ _____ _____ %	$ _____ _____ %
	$ _____ _____ %	$ _____ _____ %	$ _____ _____ %	$ _____ _____ %
	$ _____ _____ %	$ _____ _____ %	$ _____ _____ %	$ _____ _____ %
	$ _____ _____ %	$ _____ _____ %	$ _____ _____ %	$ _____ _____ %
	$ _____ _____ %	$ _____ _____ %	$ _____ _____ %	$ _____ _____ %
	$ _____ _____ %	$ _____ _____ %	$ _____ _____ %	$ _____ _____ %
	$ _____ _____ %	$ _____ _____ %	$ _____ _____ %	$ _____ _____ %
	$ _____ _____ %	$ _____ _____ %	$ _____ _____ %	$ _____ _____ %
	$ _____ _____ %	$ _____ _____ %	$ _____ _____ %	$ _____ _____ %
TOTAL	$ _____ _____ %	$ _____ _____ %	$ _____ _____ %	$ _____ 100%

Step 4—Identify the Industries, Class of Buyer or Channels of Distribution That You Will Sell Your Product/Service Into

If an industry cut is important to your business, use this worksheet:

Product: _____	Geography _____	Geography _____	Geography _____	Geography _____	Total Revenue
Industry:	$_____ _____% Avg. Sale Price = $_____ # of Sales Needed = _____	$_____ _____% Avg. Sale Price = $_____ # of Sales Needed = _____	$_____ _____% Avg. Sale Price = $_____ # of Sales Needed = _____	$_____ _____% Avg. Sale Price = $_____ # of Sales Needed = _____	$_____ _____%
Industry:	$_____ _____% Avg. Sale Price = $_____ # of Sales Needed = _____	$_____ _____% Avg. Sale Price = $_____ # of Sales Needed = _____	$_____ _____% Avg. Sale Price = $_____ # of Sales Needed = _____	$_____ _____% Avg. Sale Price = $_____ # of Sales Needed = _____	$_____ _____%
Industry:	$_____ _____% Avg. Sale Price = $_____ # of Sales Needed = _____	$_____ _____% Avg. Sale Price = $_____ # of Sales Needed = _____	$_____ _____% Avg. Sale Price = $_____ # of Sales Needed = _____	$_____ _____% Avg. Sale Price = $_____ # of Sales Needed = _____	$_____ _____%

If a class of buyer (i.e., consumer, small businesses, large corporations) cut is important to your business, use this worksheet:

Product: _____	Geography _____	Geography _____	Geography _____	Geography _____	Total Revenue
Class of buyer:	$_____ _____% Avg. Sale Price = $_____ # of Sales Needed = _____	$_____ _____% Avg. Sale Price = $_____ # of Sales Needed = _____	$_____ _____% Avg. Sale Price = $_____ # of Sales Needed = _____	$_____ _____% Avg. Sale Price = $_____ # of Sales Needed = _____	$_____ _____%
Class of buyer:	$_____ _____% Avg. Sale Price = $_____ # of Sales Needed = _____	$_____ _____% Avg. Sale Price = $_____ # of Sales Needed = _____	$_____ _____% Avg. Sale Price = $_____ # of Sales Needed = _____	$_____ _____% Avg. Sale Price = $_____ # of Sales Needed = _____	$_____ _____%
Class of buyer:	$_____ _____% Avg. Sale Price = $_____ # of Sales Needed = _____	$_____ _____% Avg. Sale Price = $_____ # of Sales Needed = _____	$_____ _____% Avg. Sale Price = $_____ # of Sales Needed = _____	$_____ _____% Avg. Sale Price = $_____ # of Sales Needed = _____	$_____ _____%

If a channel of distribution (i.e., internal sales force, resellers, etc.) cut is important to your business, use this worksheet:

Product: _____	Geography _____	Geography _____	Geography _____	Geography _____	Total Revenue
Channel of distribution:	$_____ _____% Avg. Sale Price = $_____ # of Sales Needed = _____	$_____ _____% Avg. Sale Price = $_____ # of Sales Needed = _____	$_____ _____% Avg. Sale Price = $_____ # of Sales Needed = _____	$_____ _____% Avg. Sale Price = $_____ # of Sales Needed = _____	$_____ _____%
Channel of distribution:	$_____ _____% Avg. Sale Price = $_____ # of Sales Needed = _____	$_____ _____% Avg. Sale Price = $_____ # of Sales Needed = _____	$_____ _____% Avg. Sale Price = $_____ # of Sales Needed = _____	$_____ _____% Avg. Sale Price = $_____ # of Sales Needed = _____	$_____ _____%
Channel of distribution:	$_____ _____% Avg. Sale Price = $_____ # of Sales Needed = _____	$_____ _____% Avg. Sale Price = $_____ # of Sales Needed = _____	$_____ _____% Avg. Sale Price = $_____ # of Sales Needed = _____	$_____ _____% Avg. Sale Price = $_____ # of Sales Needed = _____	$_____ _____%

DESCRIBE YOUR PROSPECTS

- Identify *whom* you will be selling to, *by title*:

TITLE

Decision maker   _____

Financial approver   _____

Technical evaluator   _____

Recommender   _____

Approver   _____

Champion   _____

Describe the factors that will help you qualify prospects (revenue, number of employees, profits, number of locations, budget, etc.):

_____

_____

Describe where the prospects are located (territory, city, state/province, country, worldwide):

_____

_____

Describe which industries or segments are the best prospects, or describe other factors that might influence your strategy (industries, your installed base, a competitive installed base, etc.):

_____

_____

_____

Based on the above, who is *most* critical to your success? (usually the ultimate decision maker is the most important and should be the focal point of your selling efforts):
Title: _____

List the secondary target(s) of your sales and marketing strategy:
Title: _____
Title: _____

BUYING CYCLE WORKSHEETS

WHAT DO YOU ULTIMATELY WANT THE CUSTOMER TO DO?

Describe your short-term and long-term goals for these prospects:

Short-term goals (e.g., buy a pilot, evaluate the product, buy an evaluation, buy the product):

_____

_____

_____

Long-term goals (e.g., become a good reference account, repeat buy, etc.):

_____

_____

_____

Describe the major checkpoints, or buying actions, the typical prospect will take to move through the Buying Cycle:

Actions

_____

_____

_____

_____

_____

Customer Buying Cycle Worksheet

For Title: _____

Total Revenue: _____

Period Beginning: _____

Period Ending: _____

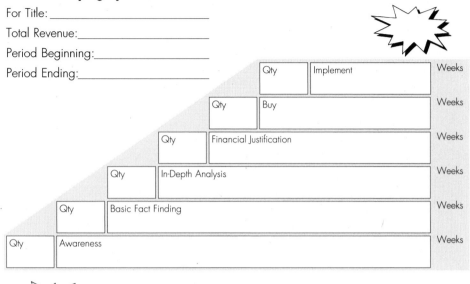

Qty	Implement	Weeks
Qty	Buy	Weeks
Qty	Financial Justification	Weeks
Qty	In-Depth Analysis	Weeks
Qty	Basic Fact Finding	Weeks
Qty	Awareness	Weeks

TRB Consulting Group, Inc. ©1994

SALES CYCLE WORKSHEETS

BUY/SELL CYCLE   Stage _____

Target audience title:

_____

_____

_____

Number of people in audience:

_____

(How many are you starting with at this point?)

Action you want the audience to take to move forward in the
Buying Cycle:

_____

_____

_____

Number of people needed to take this action:

_____

CREATING POWERFUL SALES MESSAGES

Customer Business Environment	Customer Business and Personal Needs	Features/ Characteristics of Your Product	Your Competitive Advantage	Impact on Customer's Business
_____	_____	_____	_____	_____
_____	_____	_____	_____	_____
_____	_____	_____	_____	_____
_____	_____	_____	_____	_____
_____	_____	_____	_____	_____
_____	_____	_____	_____	_____
_____	_____	_____	_____	_____

Sales and Marketing Mix Analysis

List the different ways you can communicate your sales messages to your prospects (trade shows, direct mail, seminars, etc.).
Be creative. Once you complete the list, calculate the ROI for each possibility.

Sales and Marketing Activity (trade shows, seminars, etc.)	Quantity Required (No. of people)	No. of People Who Will Act (projected) (C)	Material Prep and Delivery Costs (D)	Total Sales Costs (E)	Total Costs (columns D + E) = (F)	ROI (column F ÷ column C)

(1) From the worksheet on the following page.
(2) Sales cost calculation = number of sales calls required (add all sales, tech support, management calls) × avg. cost per call.
Example: 6 calls @ $400/call (loaded average) = $2,400 sales cost

Evaluate your alternatives *before* you decide.

SALES AND MARKETING MIX COST PROJECTION

Describe the activity/tool (e.g., sales calls, brochures, seminars, direct mail):

_____

Quantity required: _____

Projected results: _____

Estimate the cost of: _____

	Time	$
Preparation	_____	_____
Sales call(s) (1)	_____	_____
Mail	_____	_____
Telephone	_____	_____
Event costs	_____	_____
Facilities	_____	_____
Materials design and creation	_____	_____
Production costs	_____	_____
Advertising costs	_____	_____
Fulfillment	_____	_____
Toll-free number	_____	_____
Business reply card	_____	_____
Materials	_____	_____
Total fulfillment	_____	_____
Other costs	_____	_____
Total cost projection	_____	_____

Total cost projection	_____	(a)
Projected results	_____	(b)
Projected ROI	_____	(a) ÷ (b)

(1) List all calls: sales, tech support, management, etc.

SELECT THE SALES AND MARKETING MIX

Choose the sales and marketing mix that you believe will be successful. Experiment with new techniques. Determine, in advance, how you will track what is working and what isn't working.

Sales and Marketing Mix	Quantity of Results Required	What Needs to Be Tracked	How	What This Will Tell Me

CARRY OUT THE EFFORT

This worksheet completes the project planning table and identifies the following factors.

- Actions: Which actions need to be taken?
- Time line: How long will it take?
- Due date: When is it due?
- Assignments: By whom?

Actions That Need to Be Taken	How Long Will It Take	When Due	By Whom*

*Note that when any other organization within your company is called upon to take an action, its participation should be mapped out in terms of its role in the customer's Buying Cycle. It would be considered another audience, and as such, its role must be defined. See Chapter 8, "How to Deal with Multiple Audiences," for more information on mapping out multiple audiences.

Evaluation and Improvement Tool

Number of Results Achieved	Total Cost of each Sales and Marketing Mix Selection	Cost per Result	Sales and Marketing Mix +/−	Sales Messages +/−

SALES AND MARKETING SELF-HEALTH TEST

Before we begin to get in depth on the methodology, you might want to take the following Sales and Marketing Self-Health Test. See how your organization scores.

Instructions: Use this test to determine the health of your Sales and Marketing organizations. If your company is small and you do not have formal Sales and Marketing organizations, answer the questions from a functional point of view.

	YES	NO
1. Do you think that you should be selling more but you are not sure why you are not?	○	○
2. Are your Sales and Marketing organizations frequently at odds with each other or not working together well on sales and marketing strategies?	○	○
3. Do you spend a lot of money on marketing activities but don't really know what to expect or how to track results?	○	○
4. Do you know what mix of products/services you need to sell in certain geographies, industries, channels of distribution or classes of buyer in order to be successful?	○	○
5. Have you taken taken each of the above revenue cuts and determined how many sales you need to make in each category in order to be successful?	○	○
6. Have you profiled your ideal customer by title, geography, size of company, industry, issues/concerns?	○	○
7. Have you analyzed your channels of distribution to determine the best fit to move your customer to buy as quickly, efficiently and cost-effectively as possible?	○	○
8. Have you analyzed your ideal customer's Buying Cycle?	○	○
9. Do you know how many customers you need at each stage of the Buying Cycle in order to be successful?	○	○
10. Do you know how long it takes a typical customer to move through his or her Buying Cycle?	○	○
11. Are your sales messages powerful and persuasive?	○	○
12. Are your Sales and Marketing organizations, as well as all channels of distribution, giving your customers the same messages?	○	○
13. Have you determined the sales and marketing activities that you will do from a return-on-investment perspective?	○	○
14. Are your Sales and Marketing organizations, as well as all channels of distribution, working with common strategies, common messages and common metrics?	○	○

	YES	NO
15. Do you know how much your sales and marketing strategy will cost compared with the revenue you expect?	○	○
16. Do you frequently experience resource constraints at the last minute that could have been avoided with a little planning?	○	○
17. Does strong teamwork exist between your Sales and Marketing organizations as well as all channels of distribution?	○	○
18. Are your sales forecasts accurate?	○	○
19. Do your salespeople get leads from Marketing but throw them away?	○	○
20. Does your Sales force have a low opinion of Marketing?	○	○
21. When leads go to alternative channels of distribution (such as partners), do you know what happens to them? Are they tracked?	○	○
22. Have you analyzed which approaches are best to use at the various stages of a customer's Buying Cycle: sales calls, direct mail, telemarketing, alternative channels?	○	○
23. Prior to implementing them do you know that your sales strategies will work?	○	○
24. Does your organization focus on the customer first and your activities second?	○	○
25. Does your company reward people for activity more than results?	○	○

Answer Key

Score yourself as follows:

Questions 1–3	NO	4 points each
Questions 4–15	YES	4 points each
Question 16	NO	4 points
Questions 17 and 18	YES	4 points each
Questions 19 and 20	NO	4 points each
Questions 21–24	YES	4 points each
Question 25	NO	4 points

If you scored 0–24:

You are probably extremely frustrated with your current Sales and Marketing organizations. Your company may be running from one activity to the next without stopping to ask yourselves why you just did what you did—what you got out of it. A change in corporate philosophy from an activities mentality to a results mentality might be needed. *The Buck Starts Here* should help you to make that shift.

If you scored 28–48:

You are probably experiencing some frustration, but you are also seeing some results in your business. You have made the first steps in analyzing what is working, what is not working and why. You probably do not have an agreed-to plan of action between your Sales and Marketing organizations. We would suggest that you focus more on the results of your Sales and Marketing organizations (Who is the customer? What is success? How do we get there from here?) and less on the activities.

If you scored 52–72:

You are definitely moving in the right direction. You probably ask yourself the right questions and just might need some tools/techniques to make your organization more effective and efficient. Your company probably takes the time to plan, but you might abandon the plan when the fires begin, so that you are starting right but not following through. This might take discipline and management commitment. The tools in *The Buck Starts Here* should help you analyze how to take a good sales and marketing strategy and turn it into a great one.

If you scored 76–92:

You are mostly there. With a little fine-tuning, you could find yourself performing way beyond your current expectations. *The Buck Starts Here* will give you some techniques and tools that you probably have not seen to date. It will help you take what you already know to work and make it better.

If you scored 93+:

You do not need this book. You are there. Congratulations! We are sure that your efforts and organizations are focused, effective and efficient.

THE BUCK STARTS HERE QUICK REFERENCE GUIDE

Return on Investment

The Buck Starts Here methodology provides you with the tools you need to build a powerful sales and marketing strategy:

1. **Business Goal Segmentation**
   - State your business goals.
   - State your revenue goals.
   - Define your target geographies.
   - Identify your target products.
   - Define the industry, class of buyer or channel of distribution to which or through which you will sell your product.
   - Determine the number of sales needed in each key segmentation in order to achieve your objectives. How many customers must buy in order for you to be successful?

2. **Identify your Target Audience**
   Specify by title, size of company, location, industry and type of buyer. Then decide on the center of the target audience. Build the customer's Buying Cycle for this set of customers.

3. **Determine the Desired Short-Term and Long-Term Goals**
   State the revenue objectives, by date, that would define success for your sales and marketing effort.

4. **Determine Customer Actions**
   Make a list of the major actions or checkpoints the target customers would take, leading them to the desired goal.

5. **Create the Customer's Buying Cycle**
   Transfer the customer's actions to the Customer's Buying Cycle Worksheet, under the appropriate stage of the Buying Cycle.

The Buck Starts Here
Understanding the Metrics

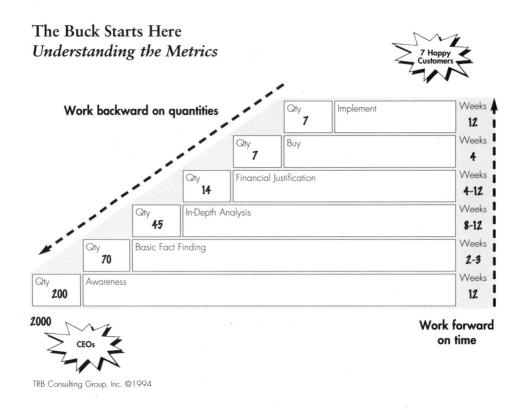

TRB Consulting Group, Inc. ©1994

6. Quantify the Number of Needed Results

Begin at the goal and decide how much of the target audience needs to reach this result in order for your sales and marketing effort to be called a success. (Relate this to your business and revenue goals.) Continue quantifying (goal down to target audience) for each stage of the Buying Cycle.

7. Determine the Elapsed Time

Estimate the elapsed time by starting at the target audience, and decide how long the typical customer would take to move from each stage of the Buying Cycle to the next. Move upward from the target audience toward the desired goal.

8. Diagnostic Capabilities

- Measure investment per result
- Identify resource constraints

- Identify results needed at each stage
- Know where to invest additional effort
- Understand integration/continuity of your sales messages
- Estimate time to reach end result

9. **Complete a Sales Cycle for each Stage of the Customer Buying Cycle**
   Completing your Sales and Marketing Operations Plan
   - Target Audience—Copy from your Customer Buying Cycle Worksheet
   - Desired Action—Choose one stage, and copy from your Customer Buying Cycle Worksheet.
   - Build Sales Messages—What is the information that is so powerful, so influential, and so motivational that people in your target audience will be compelled to take action?
   - Choose Sales and Marketing Activities—What is the best combination of sales and marketing activities that you can use to transmit your sales messages? For each sales and marketing activity, project the following information:
     — quantity required
     — projected results
     — projected cost
     — investment per result
   - Carry Out the Effort—(mini-project plan) What are the tasks you must complete, by when, to achieve the results you need?
   - Measurement Data—How will you collect the data and track your results?
   - Get Better Next Time—Look at the results you achieved; compare with previous results, if possible, and other people's results. Results come from two places: the sales messages and the sales and marketing activities. Observe what worked and what didn't. Decide how you will improve.

The Buck Starts Here gives you the capability of focusing your sales and marketing efforts on tangible and measurable results. The focus on return on investment helps Sales and Marketing to be more customer focused, more productive, better managed, more successful and more profitable.

Six Key Questions

1. Whom do you want to take action?
2. What do you want them to do?
3. What will you say to them to persuade them to take action?
4. What will you do to get them to take the action?
5. How will you know if they have done it?
6. How will you measure it?

INTEGRATE YOUR SALES AND MARKETING EFFORTS!

Example of Multiple Buy/Sell Cycles

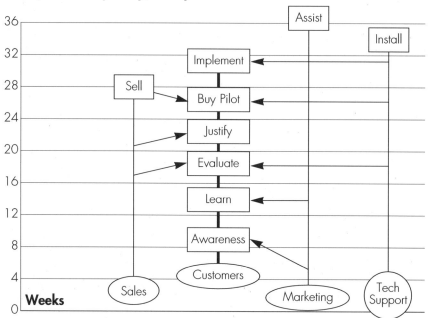

TRB Consulting Group, Inc. ©1994

Index